The Author

Dorothy Anderson was born in New Zealand, married an Englishman and has lived in the United Kingdom since 1948. Her career as a librarian began in New Zealand in what is now its National Library and she was then the first librarian of the Hendon College of Technology (as it then was). From 1959 she became increasingly involved in the work of the International Federation of Library Associations and Institutions, becoming Director of the IFLA International Office for Universal Bibliographic Control from its inception in 1971 until her retirement in 1983. It was in that position that she gained wide-ranging experience in editing and publishing as overall editor of the UBC Office's journal *'International cataloguing'* and of the many manuals and handbooks which the UBC Office published.

She has also worked as consultant for other international organizations and in this capacity has participated in meetings and specialist projects in all parts of the world. Her own professional works include two books setting out the basis of the UBC programme and its progress (1974 and 1982), manuals and guidelines prepared for Unesco, including those for cataloguing-in-publication in 1986, and in 1988 a revised edition of *Standard practices in the preparation of bibliographic records*, an overview of international work in developing bibliographic standards. She has also written historical books.

She is an Honorary Fellow of the Library Association and has received the IFLA Medal (1983) and the American Library Association Margaret Mann Citation in Cataloguing and Classification (1984).

A GUIDE TO INFORMATION SOURCES FOR THE PREPARATION, EDITING AND PRODUCTION OF DOCUMENTS

A Guide to Information Sources for the Preparation, Editing and Production of Documents

Dorothy Anderson

Gower
Aldershot · Brookfield USA · Hong Kong · Singapore · Sydney

© Dorothy Anderson 1989

All rights reserved. No part of this publication may be reproduced, stored in a retrieval system, or transmitted in any form or by any means, electronic, mechanical, photocopying, recording, or otherwise without the prior permission of Gower Publishing Company Limited.

Published by
Gower Publishing Company Limited
Gower House
Croft Road
Aldershot
Hants GU11 3HR
England

Gower Publishing Company
Old Post Road
Brookfield
Vermont 05036
USA

British Library Cataloguing in Publication Data
Anderson, Dorothy, *1923–*
   A guide to information sources for the preparation, edition and production of documents.
   1. Technical writing. Information sources
   I. Title
   808′.0666021

Library of Congress Cataloging-in-Publication Data

Anderson, Dorothy, 1923–
   A guide to information sources for the preparation, editing, and production of documents/Dorothy Anderson.
      p. cm.
      Bibliography: p. includes index.
      1. Manuscript preparation (Authorship)—Bibliography. 2. Report writing—Bibliography. 3. Editing—Bibliography. 4. Publishers and publishing—Bibliography. I. Title.
   Z5165.A3 1988
   [PN160]
   016.808′02--dc19   88–23236
                                                                  CIP
ISBN 0 566 05743 3

Printed and bound in Great Britain at
The Camelot Press Ltd, Southampton

Contents

Preface ix

Introduction xi

1 Writing the document 1
1 Introduction 1
  1.1 Scope of the chapter 1
  1.2 Summary of the chapter 2
2 Terminology 3
  2.1 The principles of terminology and methods for compiling terminological dictionaries 7
  2.2 Terminology in some specific subject fields 9
  2.3 Transliteration 11
3 The intellectual preparation of documents 12
  3.1 Preparing the written text 14
    3.1.1 Punctuation 17
    3.1.2 Quotations in the text 18
    3.1.3 Acronyms and abbreviations 19
    3.1.4 Symbols, numbers and values 22
  3.2 Preparing the written text for different types of publications 24
  3.3 Preparing the written text in specific subject fields 26
  3.4 Preparing illustrative materials 29
  3.5 Preparing and presenting spoken text 31
  3.6 Preparing for publication 34

4	Numeric data: its presentation and reporting	35
	4.1 Categories of numeric data	36
	4.2 Presenting and reporting data	37
	4.3 Standards, manuals and guidelines available for the interpretation and presentation of numeric data	38

2	**Editing the document**	**41**
1	Introduction	41
	1.1 Scope of the chapter	41
	1.2 Summary of the chapter	42
	1.3 Categories of publications	42
2	Carrying out editorial functions	46
3	Making up the publication	50
	3.1 Front matter	52
	3.2 Body of the text	57
	3.3 End matter	57
	3.4 Other descriptive and bibliographic details	60
4	Administrative aspects of editing	60
	4.1 Legal deposit requirements	64
	4.2 Copyright requirements	65
5	The editor and the publisher and printer	66
	5.1 Printing technology and typographic design	67
	5.2 Publishing and the book trade	68
	5.3 Proof reading and correction	69
6	The changing role of the editor	69

3	**Producing and publishing the document**	**73**
1	Introduction	73
	1.1 Scope of the chapter	73
	1.2 Summary of the chapter	74
2	Preparing the text for publication	75
	2.1 From typewriter to word processor	75
	2.2 Making use of a word processor	77
	2.3 Background to computers, word processors and electronic publishing	80

2.4	Standards for computers and computing applications	82
3	Producing documents on paper	85
3.1	Designing the publication	86
3.2	Choosing the paper	87
3.3	Putting the text on to paper: composition	88
3.4	Printing the document	91
3.5	Binding the document	94
4	Producing documents in microform	95
4.1	Microfilming	97
4.2	Using microforms	98
5	Producing a document with accompanying materials	99
	Postscript	101

Bibliography 103

Useful addresses 131

Author's choice 137

Index 139

Preface

This Guide is not intended for professional authors and editors, but for those in all parts of the world who, in the course of their professional lives, write articles, prepare reports, present conference papers, edit journals, organize seminars, and publish proceedings.

The dictionaries, reference books, manuals and guidelines listed and described are a selection of those available in the English language, and it is hoped that the Guide may be of value to the increasing number of authors and editors whose original languages are not English but who are planning to write or publish in that language. In many professions, and increasingly in information, science and technology, it is important in order to publicize a research project and its results that the report of that research appears in an English-language journal – a journal which may originate in North America, in India, the Netherlands, or in the United Kingdom. For such authors and editors there are strains additional to the primary ones of writing the article and finding a place for its publication: and added incentives to make use of available aids to simple English and a straightforward presentation.

The Guide is aimed at international use, albeit at authors and editors writing in the English language. As background to this intended use, some account is given of the varied and extensive work undertaken by international organizations with the aim to bring uniformity into technical vocabularies

A Guide to Information Sources for the Production of Documents

and specialist publications as part of the overall operations of standardizing manufacturing and working details. Some international organizations have standardization as their main and only task, such as the International Organization for Standardization (ISO). Others, such as Unesco through its General Information Programme (PGI) and UNISIST, have seen the advantages of uniform approaches in writing and editing as support for their basic goal of international communication. These international activities over many years and many disciplines, undertaken by many specialists, are not necessarily known to authors and editors, and the results are only apparent, and appreciated, when written technical texts become easier to read and to follow and when words used are less likely to be misunderstood or misinterpreted in translation.

To some extent this Guide is the product of such international efforts. Its origins are in work undertaken more than ten years ago by the Unesco UNISIST Working Group on Bibliographic Data Interchange which resulted in the publication in 1980 of the *UNISIST Guide to Standards for Information Handling*, a compilation which aimed to provide a framework of international standards for all activities of communicating, from writing a document to locating books on library shelves. A new version of the *UNISIST Guide* was planned with a different approach and structure, and drafts looking at the needs of author, editor and publisher were prepared. As completion of the new version is no longer planned within the current Unesco programme, the initial work which was undertaken has, with the permission of the Unesco General Information Programme, been reshaped, expanded, rewritten and updated to produce this Guide.

D.A.

London
March 1988

Introduction

Among the publications listed in the Guide are dictionaries, manuals, standards, year books and pocket guides, and their contents are as varied as their size, weight and cost in published form. Titles of some introductory texts are noted as well as references to works of academic analysis and compendia of technical information. Some of the sources are reference works of great complexity, to be found and used only in libraries. Others are available in editions suitable for purchase and the home desk. The overall aim has not been to annotate and evaluate every title, but rather to suggest a range of suitable titles of both North American and United Kingdom publications: from such a list there is the possibility, and the hope, that at least one title will be at hand in library or bookshop wherever author or editor may be.

The majority of the sources noted have been published within the past decade or have been revised, reprinted or reissued, implying that use and demand are constant. For some publications, such as dictionaries and reference handbooks, there is a continuing process of revision, and title pages are amended and contents improved regularly, even annually. It is also noticeable in the field of information technology with its unsteady vocabulary and changing equipment that publishers are fully aware of the need to produce revised up to date texts at frequent intervals. There are other publications where the contents have a continuing application, although their market value to publishers may be limited, and which have remained in print over long periods. Among these are the manuals and guidelines produced by societies and professional organizations which are not always noted in the usual book trade journals and lists, and are not available for purchase through book trade channels. A direct application to a society to purchase a handbook is usually successful, and may also reveal the existence of a more up to date version.

Also included in the Guide are references to the publications of international organizations contributing towards uniformity in communication, including ISO standards in the fields of information and documentation. It should be appreciated, however, that international standards often serve as the basis for national standards, and it is for this reason that British Standards Institution (BSI) equivalents are also listed.

Throughout the Guide references to the publications are provided in the short form of author, brief title and date of publication, with a running number in the right hand margin. The Bibliography is presented in this numerical order and the references are expanded to include sufficient information to identify the publication in a library catalogue or bookseller's list. There is an explanatory note at the beginning of the Bibliography (see p. 103).

The Guide, as well as directing the reader to existing published sources, is itself a source book. It provides the practical framework for author and editor planning for publication and explains the actions to be taken and the problems likely to be encountered, and considers the future roles of authors and editors as publishers.

1

Writing the document

1 INTRODUCTION

1.1 Scope of the chapter

The various intellectual activities involved when preparing a written text, whether it be an article, a technical report or a project survey, are the first stages in the continuing processes which end with the appearance of the text in a physical form. It is the purpose of this chapter to provide guidance to authors whereby organizing thoughts and facts is made easier; and also, in acknowledgement of the importance of today's international network of scientific and technical information, that the written text is produced in a shape that has recognized uniformity and in a style that has received international acceptance.

Language and national cultural, literary and educational traditions are the greatest influences upon all the intellectual efforts of authorship, and there can be no 'international standard' for writing, even for technical and professional documents. But the basic requirements for every document are intelligibility, conciseness and clarity of thought and expression, and the printed sources provided in this chapter may assist the author to satisfy these.

It is difficult to make a clear distinction between the steps taken by an author in preparing written text and those taken later in editing that text or preparing it for publication: some preliminary sources for the author/editor/publisher are noted, which can serve as an introduction to the full accounts presented in Chapters 2 and 3.

This chapter also covers two other topics not directly related to the preparation of documents but important in information handling: terminology and the presentation of numeric data.

Recent advances in information technology may never be fully utilized unless there is complementary development in establishing standardized terminology in specialized fields and in analysing the methodology required to create uniform terms. It is for this reason that the chapter begins with a summary of international work currently under way on terminology.

The last section of the chapter deals briefly with numeric data and its presentation in reports and surveys in such a way that it is comprehensive in explaining an experiment and comprehensible to the less than expert reader.

1.2   Summary of the chapter

2   Provides a brief account of international work in terminology and of the activities in this field of the International Organization for Standardization (ISO) and the International Information Centre for Terminology (Infoterm); the principles of terminology and related standards are noted. There is also a brief note on international work in transliteration.

3   Describes the dictionaries, manuals and guidelines which are available in the English language to assist the author. Notes are given on the special requirements for authors writing particular types of documents or in specific subject fields; and for preparing illustrations or a spoken text. Some preliminary notes for the author who is also editor and publisher lead on to Chapters 2 and 3.

4 Provides a brief account of numeric data, what it can consist of, how collected, processed, analysed; and the problems in its presentation.

2 TERMINOLOGY

Research and development in all fields of knowledge suggest not only the innovation of ideas, conclusions, but also the introduction of new terms, or of old terms with new meanings. If there is to be accurate reporting of research with a genuine communication of its results, there is the necessity to ensure that work on defining and standardizing the terms used in the research is carried on at the same time and preferably at the same speed as the research itself. But, as is very apparent at the moment, the advances of the past decade in science and technology have brought about a flood of new concepts and new terms, and the rapidity of the developments has meant evolving vocabularies with less than consistent usage. This is very familiar at the national one-language level where a new term for some piece of equipment or a new process is introduced, used uncomfortably for a while, and then is discarded or takes on a meaning quite different from its original. The speed of research developments and of changes in terms has made work on determining meanings and then creating specialist vocabularies within a single language difficult and frustrating.

Internationally trying to improve the means of communication by establishing specialist vocabularies is even more difficult because of the barriers of translation and of different language structures. Translations of words and terms, whether old and familiar or newly fabricated, cannot be reached readily without an understanding of the structure of a language and of its philosophical and cultural background. Work on terminology and on the creation of multinational vocabularies at the international level, therefore, has to deal

A Guide to Information Sources for the Production of Documents

with two necessary but distinct aspects. The first of these, the more straightforward, is:

- to establish equivalent terms in different languages relating to special terms in various scientific and technological fields.

The second aspect is the fundamental requirement:

- to study such terms and their definitions and to examine the concepts which relate to their original choice.

Work on establishing standard technical terms is carried out nationally, and sometimes regionally where one language is in use throughout a region, through organizations such as national standards institutes, specialist committees of educational and scientific associations, and professional bodies. In some countries a specialist institute may be set up for the specific purpose of language development: examples are the institute in Malaysia concerned with the development of Bahasa Malaya, in extending its vocabulary and in promoting publications in the language, and the institute attached to the University of Tanzania directed at the study of Kiswahili. As well as considering the introduction of new words, such institutions may also watch over the language and its existing structure. There is, for example, the Conseil culturel de la Communauté française with its purpose: '*la défense de la langue française*'.

The proliferation worldwide of regional organizations set up for varying political, cultural, economic or professional purposes has also meant the need for the overall development of multilingual glossaries. An example of the complexities of communication is the vocabulary produced in 1968 by the Nordic Union of Research Libraries which included library terms in the four languages of the region and in English, and with the title of its publication in Latin. Within the European Economic Community, as it has expanded its membership, there has been an urgency in establishing equivalents in more languages to satisfy the needs not only of the written words but also of the multiplicity of interpreters.

Many specialist international organizations are concerned with the development of their own specialist terminology, that is, the preferred terms established for use within a particular subject, discipline or profession. Examples are the member bodies of the International Council of Scientific Unions (ICSU), such as the International Union of Pure and Applied Chemistry (IUPAC), and the specialist agencies of the United Nations, such as the World Health Organization, with its vocabulary of the names of pharmaceutical substances. The International Electrotechnical Commission started work on specialized vocabularies as long ago as 1906 and has continued to define and elaborate terms in various languages and to publish specialized lists: one example is its two-volume multilingual dictionary of electricity published in 1983. As well as vocabularies such organizations can also develop standards relating to rules for the naming of substances.

Both nationally and internationally activities relating to terminology have increased considerably during the past decade including work on:

- the general theory of terminology (that is, basic terminological research at the national level);
- the establishment of agencies dealing with terminology and of terminological data bases;
- the application of computers in the processing of terminological data (for examples the production of vocabularies by computer).

Coordination of these activities has been undertaken through two international organizations:

- the International Organization for Standardization (ISO) and its Technical Committees (TC), in particular TC37, Terminology; and

- the International Information Centre for Terminology (Infoterm) established and supported by Unesco in the frame of its UNISIST programme.

The involvement of ISO in terminological work comes about naturally as a consequence of the scientific and technical work undertaken by its Technical Committees, each of which is concerned with standardization in a particular scientific or technical field and within a limited scope. Each Technical Committee plans to establish a basic vocabulary of its required specialized terms as a preliminary to its work of standardization. ISO has published a bibliography:

> ISO *International standard vocabularies*, 4th ed., 1986 1

listing all TC documents which include glossaries of technical terms used. ISO/TC37, Terminology, was established to coordinate all the terminological work within ISO, and has in its scope the standardization of methods for creating, compiling and setting out vocabularies, working through its SubCommittees (SC) and Working Groups (WG). ISO/TC46, Documentation, is concerned with standardizing terms in the field of documentation and information, with a Sub-Committee dealing with terminology.

Infoterm's objective is to assist in the coordination of terminological activities worldwide, and it carries out the functions:

- collecting terminological documents, particularly standardized and other specialized vocabularies;
- analysing terminological information;
- compiling bibliographies;
- advising on the application of principles in terminological work;
- preparing and producing publications on terminology;
- undertaking studies and projects on terminology;
- organizing conferences on terminological work.

A network of terminology agencies, called 'TermNet', has been established, with Infoterm acting as its coordinating centre and with its own exchange format MATER:

    ISO 6156–1987   *Magnetic tape exchange format for terminological/ lexicographical records*, 1987   2

The impact of the computer in terminological work is shown in the bibliography:

    Krommer-Benz   *International bibliography of computer assisted terminology*, 1984   3

A major publication of Infoterm:

    Felber   *Terminology manual*, 1984   4

provides a detailed account of work underway throughout the world, and of Infoterm and TermNet, as well as sections on terminological principles, projects and publications.

2.1 The principles of terminology and methods for compiling terminological dictionaries

ISO/TC37 issued in 1968–69 five recommendations and one standard which were directed at the general standardization of concepts of terms. The six documents, which are related and intended to be used together, are under revision. Draft proposals (DP) are being circulated and a new edition of the standard has been published:

    ISO 704–1987   *Principles and methods of terminology*, 1987   5

which provides an introduction to the nature of concepts, concept systems, terms and definitions; fundamental principles, applicable in any language, are presented, with the aim to facilitate the creation of new terms in any scientific or technical field.

The five draft proposals under examination are:

ISO/DP860–1987	*International unification of concepts and terms*	6
ISO/DP919–1987	*Guide for the preparation of classified vocabularies*	7
ISO/DP1087–1987	*Vocabulary of terminology*	8
ISO/DP1149–1987	*Layout of multilingual classified vocabularies*	9
ISO/DP1951–1987	*Lexicographical symbols particularly for use in classified defining vocabularies*	10

A further draft proposal complements those noted above:

ISO/DP4466–1987	*Layout of monolingual classified vocabularies*	11

Guidelines have been prepared by ISO and Unesco for establishing thesaurus, multilingual and monolingual, which are related to work on terminology but which are more directly concerned with subject analysis and classification in the field of information science.

Two other ISO standards not developed specifically for terminological work but which can be useful when working on terminological projects are:

ISO 3166–1981	*Codes for the representation of names of countries*, 2nd ed., 1981	12

with its British Standards equivalent:

BS 5374–1981	*Specification for codes for the representation of names of countries*, 1981	13

ISO/DIS639–1987   *Code for the representation of names of languages*, 1987 (DIS = Draft International Standard)   14

2.2 Terminology in some specific subject fields

A large-scale project for the preparation of multilingual vocabularies in information, documentation and librarianship was undertaken by ISO/TC46 SC3, Terminology of documentation, in 1969, and a number of parts have been published as standards and other parts issued as draft international standards (DIS):

ISO 5127–1981–3   *Documentation and information: vocabulary* Part 1, *Basic concepts*, 1983 Part 2, *Traditional documents*, 1983 Part 3a, *Acquisition, identification and analysis of documents and data*, 1981 Part 6, *Documentary languages*, 1983 Part 11, *Audio-visual documents*, 1983   15

with its British Standards equivalent published in advance of ISO:

BS 5408–1976   *Glossary of documentation terms*, 1976   16

ISO/DIS5127–1987   *Documentation and information: vocabulary*   17

> Part 3, *Iconic documents*
> Part 4, *Archival documents*
> Part 7, *Retrieval and dissemination of information*
> Part 8, *Reprography of documents*

To assist the international exchange of information in computerized form, ISO prepared a standardized vocabulary of terms used in data processing, which in various parts was issued as ISO 2382 and published together as:

> ISO   *Standards Handbook 10: Data processing: vocabulary*, 1982   18

(Revised editions of a number of the parts appeared in 1987.) *Handbook 10* complements two others, *8*, and *9*, which cover the standards for hardware and software aspects of data processing.

An overview of research and applications in multilingual information processing is provided in:

> Bennett and others   *Multilingual aspects of information technology*, 1986   19

The many specialist multilingual dictionaries available vary in relation to the number of languages included and the breadth or detail of the topics covered. Some are the products of specialist publishers, such as Elsevier; others are prepared by professional international associations; the subject range is as wide as the alphabet, from automobile engineering to yachting. The three titles listed here indicate this width of coverage.

> International Federation of Automatic Control   *Multilingual glossary*, 1981 (6 languages)   20

	The multilingual business handbook: a guide to international correspondence, 1983 (5 languages)	21
Room	*Dictionary of translated names and titles*, 1986 (6 languages)	22

Multilingual dictionaries are also listed in the text, dealing with conference organization (1.3.5); printing and the book trade (2.5.1); and computers (3.2.3.).

2.3 Transliteration

It is apparent that written communication across language barriers is easier when the same alphabet is used and the processes of translation can be identified immediately by the reader and appreciated readily. When different scripts are involved, every aspect of communication and all international work to aid communication, including that on terminology, takes longer. There is the problem of conversion to a common script, with consequent danger of losing meanings and sounds. Over a long period the solution of the conversion of scripts – transliteration – has been followed in the library world for some practices; for example, in card catalogues the bibliographic records for non-roman script publications are converted into the roman script, which permits filing the cards in one sequence and makes for easier use by readers not familiar with different scripts. Other problems have arisen because of different transliteration schemes with the resulting separation of authors' names in forms such as Cechov, Cecov, Cekof, Tchekhof, Tschechoff, for the well known Russian writer.

There are sometimes conflicting requirements between nationally developed transliteration schemes and those developed for international use, for example in building up international data bases by the merging of bibliographic records from different countries. A recent approach has been to work towards the development of two schemes for each script, one which is convertible and reconvertible for international use, and a national and/or simplified scheme.

International work in this field is carried out by ISO/TC46, Documentation, through its SubCommittee 2, Conversion of written languages, and priority has been given to romanization, that is, the conversion of non-roman scripts into the roman alphabet. A number of standards and draft proposals have been prepared covering Slavic, Cyrillic, Arabic, Hebrew and Greek characters, and work is also under way for non-Slavic, Cyrillic, Japanese, Yiddish, Chinese and Korean scripts. Available ISO standards are grouped together in:

ISO *Standards Handbook 1: Information transfer*, 2nd ed., 1982 23

It is apparent that these international schemes cover only a very small portion of the scripts in use worldwide, and many schemes first created for national use are accepted internationally. A very significant governmental decision was that taken in China in 1979 to adopt a 'pin yin' conversion scheme instead of the old established Wade-Giles or Yale: which is why the once familiar 'Peking' has now to be recognized as 'Beijing'.

In some multilingual multiscript countries, rather than transliterate, every effort is made to maintain the equality of the languages, and all public signs and documents appear in all languages and scripts, and in catalogues and data base records different scripts are merged; this, for example, is the practice in Singapore.

3 THE INTELLECTUAL PREPARATION OF DOCUMENTS

For every author the main concern is to write in such a way

Writing the Document

that the text, whether prepared as an article, as a textbook, as a conference paper or as a technical research report, will be understood by its readers.

It is not always easy to be certain of that understanding and many factors can hinder the flow of communication between author and reader: the subject matter may require a limited and very specific vocabulary; the style may have been adjusted to suit a particular kind of reader; the text may have been written for spoken presentation and then re-written for publication; and there is also the additional and very personal factor of trying to write in a way that will be sufficiently clear and alive to hold the attention of readers or listeners.

Whatever the demands upon the author of subject matter, language, style, type of publication, the same basic steps in the preparation of the written text will have been taken:

- collecting the material which is to make up the contents of the written document;
- organizing that material into a logical and coherent framework;
- elaborating that framework from introduction through to conclusions or final summary;
- writing the document;
- arranging the written text into a manuscript ready for publication.

The first four steps are considered in this chapter. The fifth, and further steps taken after writing the document and before its publication, are discussed in Chapter 2.

Authors differ greatly in the style of their writing even when the content of a document is straightforward and its purpose as mundane as a project report. When, from the nature of the subject matter, the text is complex in content or abstract or theoretical in argument, there are likely to be even greater variations in authors' sentence structure and vocabulary. There are, however, some well defined and very basic principles relating to style and word usage which, well estab-

A Guide to Information Sources for the Production of Documents

lished and universally acknowledged over a long period, have almost reached the status of a kind of 'international standard'; and have equal relevance in structuring written text clearly whatever its language. In the English language such principles have been set out and then expanded in a number of guidelines and manuals which have become traditionally the basic 'tools of the trade' for every author writing in English. There is indeed a wealth of advice available in a wide range of publications and a selection of the best known and most useful are listed in this chapter. All start with the first principle: 'Think what you want to say; then say it as simply as possible.'

3.1 Preparing the written text

Most authors over a period make up their own selection of reference books and manuals which they like to have at hand for consultation or to boost confidence. The selection will usually include dictionaries, guides to word selection, manuals of word usage, perhaps a grammar of language, an encyclopaedia, a collection of quotations. The choice of such working tools is very personal, determined by such factors as ease of handling (that is, a one-volume dictionary rather than a larger multi-volume set); easy to see clear print; up to date with new terms; following American rather than British word usage (or vice-versa); paperback and cheaper in price. In addition, for the author writing in a specialist subject field, there will be the need for specialist glossaries, reference books, and that one and only essential handbook which seems to exist in every scientific and technical field.

(This author's preferred selection is listed at the end of the book.)

Dictionaries The list of dictionaries given here is a small selection of the many that are available and includes some of the well known established titles. All of these are in a continuing state of reprinting and/or revision and later editions than those noted here may have already appeared. Most dictionaries are published in a variety of bindings, to suit all purposes and pockets, such as luxury, standard, paperback. It is also usual for variant or sub-sets of the full edition to be published, with such titles as concise, compact, pocket, handy. For writing purposes a pocket or handy edition is likely to prove inadequate; on the other hand, a concise edition in one volume in paperback may well suit the needs of many authors.

> *Chambers 20th century dictionary*, 1987   24
> *The concise Oxford dictionary*, 1987   25
> *The new Collins concise dictionary*, 1987   26
> *Webster's new collegiate dictionary*, 1987   27

It is worth remembering that the larger editions of dictionaries, as well as the main alphabetical sequence, include appendices of 'useful information' such as tables of dates, weights and measures, names and symbols, conversion tables, lists of rulers, presidents, prime ministers, which considerably extend their function. From this point of view there are advantages in working with a dictionary the scope of which is wide enough to be both dictionary and concise encyclopaedia:

> *The Oxford reference dictionary*, 1986   28

includes brief entries for topics from art through to sport, with concise biographies and illustrations.

The best known of the dictionaries designed to aid word selection is:

> *Roget's Thesaurus*, 1987   29

which, since it was first published in 1852, has been continuously revised and updated. It is an aid to vocabulary building, with words and phrases arranged according to ideas rather than in an alphabetical sequence. A complementary dictionary to *Roget's Thesaurus* is:

> *The Penguin modern guide to synonyms and related words*, 1987   30

which defines, explains and distinguishes words of similar but not identical meaning.

A dictionary with its contents directed at the needs of authors is:

> *The Oxford dictionary for writers and editors*, 1986   31

Style manuals Most of the manuals listed here are old established 'classics' in English usage which have maintained their value over a long period, often reprinted and sometimes revised.

Fowler	*A dictionary of modern English usage*, 1987	32
Partridge	*Usage and abusage*, 1982 (designed to supplement and complement Fowler)	33
Gowers	*The complete plain words*, 1986	34
Phythian	*A concise dictionary of correct English*, 1987 (based on Fowler, Gowers, and others)	35
Strunk	*The elements of style*, 1982	36
Todd	*International English usage*, 1986	37

The 'style manuals' compiled by a publisher or professional association in order to standardize the design of their own publications usually cover the functions of both writing and editing, with stipulations of layout, style of references, etc., and are listed in Chapter 2.

Style manuals include discussions and decisions on various grammatical points but do not aim to be comprehensive in covering English grammar. Two dictionaries directed at assisting sentence construction and grammar are:

    Cowie   *Oxford dictionary of current*   38
                           idiomatic English, 1985 2v.
                           vol. 1, *Verbs with*
                           prepositions and
                           participles
                           vol. 2, *Phrase, clause*
                           and sentence idioms
    Oxford guide to the English language, 1985   39
                           Part 1, *The Oxford guide to*
                           English usage (grammar,
                           pronunciation, word forms)
                           Part 2, *Dictionary*

For the author who would like to have at hand a grammar textbook the standard but large work is:

    Quirk   *A grammar of contemporary*   40
                           English, 1987

or two less bulky books based on the above:

    Leech   *A communicative grammar of*   41
                           English, 1987
    Quirk   *A university grammar of*   42
                           English, 1987

3.1.1 Punctuation

Styles of punctuation and the punctuation symbols used vary greatly from country to country and language to language, and even within a country or language it is rare to find two authors who use punctuation in the same way. There are rules about the purpose and use of each punctuation symbol, but most authors make their own choice of what, where and how to use the symbols. Differences in punctuation usage are even more noticeable in bibliographies, references, footnotes, and abbreviations (see 1.3.1.3). It is for this reason that publishers and editors of collective works such as conference papers try to establish a consistent 'house style' of punctuation with stipulations and rules presented to their authors.

Most of the manuals listed at 1.3.1 include sections on punctuation. Two additional sources to the rules of punctuation are:

    Carey   *Mind the stop*, 1986   43
    Partridge   *You have a point there*, 1983 44

Punctuation marks can also be used with special or symbolic meanings, as in formulae, equations and codes. In the bibliographic records found in library catalogues punctuation is used within the record to indicate specific functions, and particular punctuation marks are used in accordance with cataloguing rules and are known as 'prescribed punctuation' which can be read by the computer as well as by the library user. For example, in accordance with the Anglo-American Cataloguing Rules (AACR2), which are in use in the majority of libraries in English-language countries, the slash symbol (/) indicates that what follows is the name of the author. The Bibliography of this book (see p. 103) makes use of 'prescribed punctuation' to differentiate the parts of each entry.

3.1.2 Quotations in the text

When introducing quotations into the text, the author wants to make sure that the quoted words, phrases or sentences are easily recognized, either by isolating the quotation with punctuation marks, or by indentation or the use of smaller type. How this is best done depends on the length of the quoted piece: a short quotation, less than three lines in typescript, can be incorporated into the text and distinguished

Writing the Document

with punctuation marks; three lines or more is better displayed as an indented paragraph, perhaps making use of smaller type. There are also variations in the punctuation marks used to isolate the quotation: the choice of single or double quotation marks, apostrophes, or raised commas can be a personal or editorial decision.

Authors making use of substantial quotations or of copied or re-drawn illustrations must ensure that they have obtained permission from the original author or publisher: see Chapter 2 for notes on copyright.

3.1.3 Acronyms and abbreviations

Within every profession there are well known organizations and widely used documents, standards, phrases, all of which are commonly referred to by initials or by an acronym made up of the initials of the group of words which are the name or title. In the field of information and documentation, for example, initials and acronyms in wide use are:

FID	International Federation for Documentation
IFLA	International Federation of Library Associations and Institutions
ISBD	International Standard Bibliographic Description
CIP	Cataloguing-in-Publication
MARC	Machine-Readable Cataloguing

These may not be recognized outside the profession; or may be confused. For example, in other circles:

IFLA	International Federation of Landscape Architects

The advantages of using acronyms in written text, which are said to be the savings in time and space for author and editor, are balanced by the disadvantages, and possible irritation, for the reader who may not know the acronym or recognize it in a particular language form. The initialism in one language can be a more easily mouthed acronym in another; for example:

ISDS   International Serials Data System (English form)
SIPS   *Système international de données sur les publications en série* (French form of name)

In lectures the use of acronyms can be very frustrating for the listener.

In writing a document in which it seems useful to use acronyms, it is essential that the first time the title is presented it is written out in full, followed in parentheses by the acronym which is to be used thereafter (see the usage followed in 1.2 in describing the activities of ISO). In a document where many acronyms have been used, it is helpful to the reader to provide an alphabetical list as an appendix.

Dictionaries of acronyms and initialisms in common use have been published, and most of the general dictionaries include lists of acronyms. There is the worry that acronyms change very frequently, some disappear, new letters are introduced, and new acronyms appear; hence, when used, dictionaries must be checked for new materials and changes in organizational titles.

    Pugh   *Dictionary of acronyms and*   45
                              abbreviations, 1987

in its revised edition covers acronyms for terms used in academic, scientific technological and political sources worldwide.

    Elsevier's foreign-language teacher's dictionary of   46
                acronyms and abbreviations,
                1985

is useful in relating initials in different languages for the same term.

Certain phrases occurring frequently in economic, social and political texts are often replaced by acronyms, but with the added confusion that the words when written in full are normally in the lower-case, appearing in the acronym as upper-case. For example:

gross national product   GNP
research and development   R & D
least developed countries LDCs

Scientific and technical abbreviations, such as symbols of chemical elements and signs such as ° (degree) and % (per cent) are used freely in scientific, economic and technical texts, presumably in the genuine expectation that they are familiar to all readers of those texts.

In some languages and in some contexts it is the practice to abbreviate words in the text itself (but not usually in English texts). It is even more common in all languages to shorten words in references, footnotes, tables, as well as in bibliographic references. For example:

   ed.   editor or edition
   illus. illustrated or illustrations
   vol.   volume

It is also common to abbreviate titles of publications in bibliographic references, especially serial titles. The bibliographic records of serial articles provided by indexing and abstracting services usually show the title of the serial in which the article can be found in a truncated form. This usage is economic, provided that the truncated form shown identifies a serial title uniquely. To satisfy this special criterion, an international standard has been developed and is in widespread use:

   ISO 4–1984   *Rules for the abbreviation of*   47
                      title words and titles of
                      publications, 1984

and the British Standards equivalent:

   BS 4148–1985   *Specifications for the*   48
                         abbreviation of title words
                         and titles of publications,
                         1985

The rules established can be applied to titles of serials and non-serial publications in Italic, Germanic, Balto-Slavic, Hellenic, Ural-Altaic languages. The International Serials Data System (ISDS), which is responsible for the allocation of the unique identifying number, the International Standard Serial Number (ISSN), to serial titles published all over the world, also creates a short bibliographic record for each serial title. In the ISDS records, a formulated 'key title' which is unique to each serial is used, and then that 'key title' is abbreviated in accordance with the rules of ISO 4.

The ISDS records are published in the ISDS Register (some 400,000 serial titles at the end of 1987), and in addition ISDS maintains ISO 4 and publishes, as an aid to identification, a list of serial titles in their abbreviated form:

| ISDS | *List of serial title word abbreviations*, 1985 | 49 |

For further details about ISDS and the allocation of ISSN, see Chapter 2.

In some disciplines acronyms have become widely accepted code-words and are recommended for use as such internationally. As an example, DNA is in use for deoxyribonucleic acid as well as the French ADN (for desoxyribonucleique) and the German DNS (for Desoxyribonukleinsäure). On the other hand, for many substances in use in industry, medicine and agriculture, short popular names now exist and are superseding traditional acronyms.

3.1.4 Symbols, numbers and values

The use of symbols and units of measurement in particular types of documents or in parts of documents, such as tables, presents something of the same advantages and disadvantages as the use of acronyms and abbreviations: but with the added advantages that the saving in space is the greater because of the difficulty and length in expressing some measurements

Writing the Document

and that the reader's eye more readily accepts mathematical type symbols than acronyms. Similarly with the presentation of numbers within a written text.

Traditional conventions decree that numbers can be expressed in figures or spelt out in words, and the nature of the text is the usual determining factor. It is usual to write out numbers in legal documents and when the style is narrative or literary – making a generous exception for dates. In scientific and technical texts numbers are used almost exclusively; and, naturally enough, in statistical documents. Editorial style manuals give detailed specifications on when and how to select words, numbers, symbols, etc.; see Chapter 2.

Standards have been prepared in some specialist subject fields to unify and make available for easy and accurate translation the quantities, units and symbols in use in those subjects.

Among the international standards are:

ISO 31	which consists of 13 separate parts for quantities, units and symbols in special subject fields, including:
ISO 31/1–1978	*Quantities and units of space and time*
ISO 31/11–1978	*Mathematical signs and symbols for use in physical sciences and technology*
ISO 1000–1981	*SI units and recommendations for the use of their multiples and of certain other units*
	The SI units, adopted for international use under the Système International d'Unité, are now used for all scientific and most technical purposes. The seven fundamental units are: metre, kilogram, second, ampere, kelvin, candela, mole.

These international standards are published together in:

| ISO | *Standards Handbook 2: Units of measurement,* 1982 | 50 |

23

The British Standards equivalent of ISO 31 is:

BS 5775–1979–82   13 parts   51

The international standard for the symbols and vocabulary used in presenting statistical information is ISO 3534–1977 which can be found with other standards relating to statistical methods in:

ISO   *Standards Handbook 3:*   52
                   Statistical methods, 1981

Also of relevance are:

ISO 4217–1987   *Codes for the representation*   53
                   of currencies and funds, 1987
ISO 3166–1981   *Codes for the representation*   12
                   of names of countries, 1981
ISO/DIS639–1987   *Codes for the representation*   14
                   of names of languages

The International Union of Pure and Applied Chemistry, working through its various specialist commissions, including its Commission for Symbols, Units and Nomenclatures, has published various specialist lists, usually as appendices to issues of its *Information Bulletin*. These lists cover definitions, symbols, units and their usage, terminology, with recommendations for usage in subjects such as colloid chemistry, mass spectrometry, biochemistry.

In the fields of electronics and electrical engineering the International Electrotechnical Commission has prepared and produced standards on the letter symbols to be used in electrical technology and the graphic symbols to be used in diagrams, charts, tables.

3.2 Preparing the written text for different types of publications

The author, when writing a particular type of document, such as a journal article, or for an occasion such as a conference, may be provided with guidelines directly from the editor concerned with the journal or the conference. Such guidelines can cover every aspect of the writing, from its style, vocabulary, length and structure, to editorial 'house style' details of numbering of heading and layout of references: see also Chapter 2. The suggestions and recommendations provided in the general style manuals listed in 1.3.1 are relevant whatever the type of document, but there are also manuals directed at the particular problems of planning and writing some special types of publications. Because of the interest in communicating research clearly and unambiguously, there has been an interest in trying to create a uniform structure for reports and theses, and international standards are available:

ISO 5966–1982 *Presentation of scientific and technical reports*, 1982   54

ISO 7144–1986 *Presentation of theses and similar documents*, 1986   55

and the British Standard equivalent:

BS 4821–1972 (1986) *Recommendation for the presentation of theses*   56

ISO 215–1986 *Presentation of contributions to periodicals and other serials*, 1986   57

and the British Standard equivalent:

BS 2509–1970 (1983) *Specification for the presentation of serial publications including periodicals* (also incorporates ISO 8, *Presentation of periodicals*)   58

Manuals concerned with reports, research papers, etc., include:

Booth	*Writing a scientific paper,* 1978	59
Mathes	*Designing technical reports,* 1976	60
Mitchell	*How to write reports,* 1974	61
Mort	*How to write a successful report,* new ed., 1984	62
Sussams	*How to write effective reports,* 1983	63
Turabian	*A manual for writers of research papers, theses and dissertations,* 1982	64

3.3 Preparing the written text in specific subject fields

The author writing in a specific subject field is likely to be knowledgeable, and is probably expert, in that field, and hence is aware of the problems that will arise in preparing a written text. First, related to content, are the questions of vocabulary and intended readership: an article in a very specialized journal can use a limited vocabulary with highly technical terms, but widening the audience implies broadening the vocabulary and probably expanding the text. In some subject fields tables, charts, maps and graphs are necessary and inevitable parts of the contents: again the reader with the same professional background will be familiar with styles of layout, wording of captions and abbreviations: for a wider readership the author may need to redesign graphs and rethink captions. The end result of such an exercise could well be an improvement in clarity and simplicity which will be appreciated by the expert as well as the general readers.

In addition to the general dictionaries and style manuals noted in 1.3.1, for the technical author there are subject dictionaries, specialist handbooks and the style manuals specially prepared for authors writing in specific subject fields.

Dictionaries The wide range of specialist dictionaries include some which are very limited in scope and vocabulary, such as in the field of electronics, and others, as with economics, where the vocabulary covered is wide, almost unlimited. The value of such dictionaries is in assisting with definitions of terms and with their differing usage; for example between terms used in North America and in other English language countries. In using such reference tools, it is essential to make sure that the contents are up to date; that is, that the dictionary is in a continuous state of revision.

Examples of specialized up to date English language dictionaries are:

	The ALA glossary of library and information science, 1983	65
	Harrod's librarians' glossary and reference book of terms used in librarianship, documentation and the book crafts, 6th ed., 1987	66
Isaacs	*The Penguin dictionary of science*, 6th ed., 1986	67
Stiegler	*Dictionary of economics and business*, 2nd ed., 1985	68

A comprehensive specialist dictionary is:

Chambers' science and technology dictionary, new ed., 1984   69

Typical of the small 'pocket' specialized dictionaries which can be used to supplement a larger general dictionary is:

Horner	*Newnes pocket dictionary of business terms*, 1984	70

Style manuals Professional associations and organizations have been in the forefront in producing manuals as guidance for authors writing in specific subject fields or for specific journals. These manuals usually include stipulations on presentation as well as advice on planning and writing an article or report, advice which is just as helpful to the non-technical author. For example:

O'Connor	*Writing scientific papers in English*, 1978	71

which was originally sponsored by the International Union of Geological Sciences and Editerra and is published by Pitman Medical Books.

Other manuals addressed to the technical author include:

Booth	*Communicating in science: writing and speaking*, 1985	72
Calnan	*Writing medical papers*, 1973	73
King	*Why not say it clearly? A guide to scientific writing*, 1978	74
Kirkman	*Good style for scientific and engineering writing*, 1980	75
Thorne	*Better medical writing*, 2nd ed., rev., 1977	76
Trelease	*How to write scientific and technical papers*, 1969	77

It is perhaps a reflection on the limited market for these manuals that, although some were published more than ten years ago, they are still in print. Some of the style manuals produced by professional associations are available through the usual book trade channels, marketed for a wider audience than just the association members and authors; many appear also to have a long life in print. Some examples, covering American and British usage, are:

American Institute of Physics	*Style manual*, 3rd ed., 1978	78

American Psychological Association	*Publication manual*, 2nd ed., 1974	79
Council of Biology Editors	*Style manual*, 4th ed., 1978	80
Royal Society	*General notes on the preparation of scientific papers*, 3rd ed., 1974	81
Modern Humanities Research Association	*Style book*, 3rd ed., 1986	82

3.4 Preparing illustrative materials

The technical author may find it useful, or even essential, to supplement the written text with illustrative material which can be very specific to the subject – for example, statistical tables, flow charts, maps – or can be the more usual types of illustrations, such as line drawings or photographs. In some contexts, it is certain, a graph can present a conclusion more dramatically than words, and tables make detailed comparisons of numbers and quantities easier to follow than complex phrases.

The responsibility for preparing and producing the illustrative material to accompany written text rests with the author, and ideally the selection of the illustrations should be part of the planning preparations of the whole document in order to produce a coherent and complete account. Consultation with editor or printer may help, particularly with suggestions on the easiest and most economical ways of incorporating illustrations into the text.

Some manuals have been produced addressed to the particular problems of illustrative materials with text. Examples are:

Hartley	*Designing instructional text*, 2nd ed., 1985	83

Pickens	*The copy-to-press handbook: preparing words and art for print*, 1985	84
White	*Editing by design*, 2nd ed., 1982	85
Wood	*Scientific illustration*, new ed., 1982	86

Some of the manuals listed at 3.3 above include chapters dealing with the presentation of illustrative materials: for example:

line drawings	in Booth	72
half tone illustrations	in Royal Society	81
graphs	in O'Connor	71
tables	in O'Connor; Booth	71, 72

Many of the editorial style manuals which deal with typescript and printed presentation (and which are described more fully in Chapter 2) include rules for the design and layout of illustrative materials. The United Nations manual, for example:

United Nations	*UN editorial manual*, 1983	87

has a detailed chapter on tables setting out rules which deal with the relationship between items listed vertically and horizontally, and includes a glossary of the special terms used in creating tables.

The International Electrotechnical Council has prepared standards and recommendations for electrical drawings and for the symbols and conventions used in those drawings (see also 1.3.1.4). The specialist Commissions of the International Union of Pure and Applied Chemistry have produced recommendations for graphs, their nomenclature and the signs to be used (see also 1.3.1.4).

Very specific international standards for technical drawings have been developed by the ISO Technical Committees, TC10, Technical drawings, and TC145, Graphic symbols. An important aspect of these standards has been the establishment of accepted conventions for the graphic symbols to be used. For convenience these standards are brought together in:

    ISO   *Standards Handbook 12:*   88
                        Technical drawings, 1982

The international standards for the symbols to be used on maps were prepared by ISO/TC82, Mining:

    ISO 710 1974–84   *Graphical symbols for use on*   89
                                detailed maps, plans and
                                geological cross-sections, 7
                                parts, 1974–84

Specifications for the flow charts used in information processing are set out in international standards which are brought together in:

    ISO   *Standards Handbook 9: Data*   90
                        processing: software, 1982

3.5 Preparing and presenting spoken text

There can, and should be, considerable differences between the text presented as a lecture or given verbally at a conference and written text intended primarily for reading. The extent of the differences will reflect the lecturer's/author's personality, manner of speaking, and physical stance, as well as matters relating to the communication between lecturer and audience through sounds and possibly pictures, that is, the spoken word with some accompanying visual aids.

    The basic criteria for the preparation of a spoken paper, however, are identical with those required for the written, with the emphasis on clear expression and coherent thought. Presenting a paper verbally makes additional demands upon the author, which can be physically and mentally exhausting.

A Guide to Information Sources for the Production of Documents

To assist the lecturer/author/speaker a number of guides and manuals are available, including:

Dunckel	*The business guide to effective speaking*, 1985	91
Janner	*Complete speechmaker*, 2nd ed., 1986	92

Two manuals addressed at the problems of a particular topic and a special audience are:

Calnan	*Speaking at medical meetings*, 2nd ed., 1981	93
Dixon	*Talking about your research*, 1981	94

The successful presentation of papers at meetings is very closely related to the successful organization of the meeting itself: for example, whether the organizers are able to provide clear guidance to speakers about papers and presentation, with details of length required, type and size of expected audience, the intention or not to publish the papers, the availability of aids for illustrating the spoken text. The author, after preparing a paper for spoken presentation, can be disappointed and dismayed by its appearance in print in an unchecked unedited form; although it is more usual for an author to be given the opportunity to edit and even rephrase the original spoken words. The number of professional conferences and seminars has increased steadily and so has the range of manuals and guides dealing with their organization, including:

Drain	*Successful conference and convention planning*, 1978	95
Jax	*Blueprint for success: a manual for conventions, conferences, seminars*, 1981	96
Loughary	*Producing workshops*,	97

Writing the Document

	seminars and short courses, 1979	
Lowry-Corry	*Let's have a conference*, 1987	98
Seekings	*How to organize effective conferences and meetings*, 3rd ed., 1987	99

Aids in the organization of multilingual conferences are two manuals produced by the International Association of Professional Conference Organizers and by Unesco:

IAPCO	*Glossary of conference terminology*, 1980	100

provides terms in five languages (English, German, French, Spanish, Italian) to assist in the preparation of a conference manual.

Unesco	*Glossary of conference terms*, 2nd ed., 1980	101

provides terms used in conference procedures in three languages (English, French, Arabic).

It is useful, and may even be necessary, to have at hand a guide on the formal rules of procedure for meetings, such as:

	Citrine's ABC of chairmanship, 4th ed., 1982	102

A guide to the use of audio-visual aids in library science teaching, which has been produced by Unesco for worldwide use, also includes chapters on the use of audio-visual aids generally:

Thompson	*Guide to the production and use of audio-visual aids in library and information science teaching*, 1983	103

A more comprehensive manual, also directed at library use, is:

Cullen *Design and production of* 104
         media presentations for
         libraries, 1986

3.6 Preparing for publication

It is becoming increasingly common for the author, while preparing the written text, to be planning to undertake the complementary roles of editor and even publisher. Chapters 2 and 3 cover the practical organizational details of editing and producing a document, but as a conclusion to this section, which has been concerned with the author and the intellectual preparation of text, some handbooks and manuals are listed which could provide background for the author looking towards publication. These are not style manuals, but, as guides to the book trade and to publishing, they provide information on current trends, markets, advice on copyright, etc.

Among the general yearbooks and guides are:

The book publishing annual: highlights, analyses, trends 105

Taubert *The book trade of the world*, 4v. 106

Willing's press guide 107

Guides written specifically for the author are:

Legat *An author's guide to publishing*, new ed., 1987 108

Wells *The successful author's handbook*, 1981 109

and for the author as publisher:

Finch *How to publish yourself*, 1987 110

Many authors now prepare their texts directly for publication making use of word processors. Hence the requirements that the author, while writing the text, is also structuring its layout and is putting it physically on to paper or tape or disc; and in so doing has need of editorial guidelines and may need programming skills. Manuals and guides as aids to authors working under these new conditions are now being produced: for example:

Fluegelman	*Writing in the computer age: word processing skills and style*, 1983	111
Hammond	*The writer and the word processor*, 1984	112
Holloway	*Author-generated phototypesetting: author–publisher–printer links*, 1985	113
O'Connor	*Model guidelines for the preparation of camera-ready typescripts by authors and typists*, 1980	114

The discussion on publishing and information technology and prospects for the future in book production continues in Chapters 2 and 3.

4 NUMERIC DATA: ITS PRESENTATION AND REPORTING

Numeric data results from measurements and observations made during research and investigations: for example, from the observation of particular events, from the measurement by instruments or by automatic equipment or by remote sensors. Data investigations can be undertaken in a small laboratory with the data collected by one person and set down in a notebook; or can be the product of large cooperative international programmes, with the data communicated from automatic earth stations or from satellites.

A Guide to Information Sources for the Production of Documents

Every year many millions of items of data are collected. These have then to be processed, to be stored by transfer on to magnetic tapes, discs, films or punched cards. After collection and processing come the first steps in analysis and interpretation; that is, arranging the data so as to provide patterns and summaries. It is usually at this stage when the data is being refined and reduced that some intellectual (that is, human) checks are made in order to show up and eliminate errors that have occurred in the two previous stages.

Although numeric data can be considered more concrete than bibliographic data, it presents much greater diversity in content, is less stable, and can be represented in various ways: hence the problems of incompatibility and lack of standardization in numeric data bases and in the systems for their handling. Investigations based on data related to the same phenomenon but collected under varying conditions and processed in accordance with different practices cannot provide reliable conclusions. Incompatibility arising from such variations in data bases and their systems has proved a major obstacle to data exchange.

To overcome these obstacles a number of recommendations and standards have been prepared by international organizations directed at unifying the presentation of numeric data as far as names, symbols and definitions used to represent quantity (see also 1.3.1.4). The organizations concerned include the Committee on Data for Science and Technology (CODATA) of the International Council of Scientific Unions (ICSU), the International Union of Pure and Applied Chemistry (IUPAC), and ISO.

4.1 Categories of numeric data

An attempt to categorize scientific and technological data was undertaken by an ICSU-CODATA Task Group and is presented in:

ICSU-CODATA   *Study on the problems of*   115
                   accessibility and
                   dissemination of data for
                   science and technology, 1974

The categories listed are:

- time-independent and time-dependent data
- location-independent and location-dependent data
- primary, derived and theoretical data
- determinable and stochastic data
- quantitative and qualitative data
- data as numerical values, graphs or models.

In addition to the above categories, there are other types of data in other subject fields: for example, statistical surveys, census reports, economic indicators. Some textbooks on statistics provide recommendations on the presentation of data, its analysis and interpretation in specific subject fields.

4.2 Presenting and reporting data

The author involved in the presentation and reporting of numeric data, whether in the form of a report, an article or a chapter in a handbook, can with advantage make use of the style manuals noted in section 3 above. In addition there are the particular points related to describing the investigation and the data collected.

In reporting on the use of data as a source of information, it is important to identify and describe:

- the conditions under which the data were measured;
- the characteristics of the measuring equipment;
- the techniques used to analyse the data obtained;
- the conclusions drawn from the measurements;

in addition the report must state clearly:

- the assumptions upon which the experiment/investigation

was based and how the data were identified and collected;
- references to the standards that relate measurements to the fundamental units.

4.3 Standards, manuals and guidelines available for the interpretation and presentation of numeric data

The international standards applicable to the reporting of numeric data have been brought together in:

    ISO   *Standards Handbook 2: Units*   50
                        of measurement, 1982

and those relating to statistical methods in:

    ISO   *Standards Handbook 3:*   52
                        Statistical methods, 1981

and the British Standards equivalent:

    BS 2846–1985   *Guide to the statistical*   116
                        interpretation of data, 7 parts, 1985

The ICSU-CODATA Task Group also produced a guide published by Unesco:

    ICSU-CODATA   *Guide for the presentation in*   117
                        the primary literature of numerical data derived from experiments, 1974

A publication sponsored by CODATA and Unesco provides an overview of data handling for science and technology:

    Rossmasler   *Data handling for science and*   118
                       technology, 1980

The US National Bureau of Standards has produced a series of publications dealing with the processing and analysis of numeric data and also, in trying to establish the use of standards in the identification and classification of data, reports on the advantages and problems in setting up its Standard Reference Data Centre. However, NBS publications are not generally available through the book trade channels, but can be obtained directly from the NBS.

An account of the problems in establishing numeric data bases is given in:

Chen   *Numeric data bases*, 1984   119

2

Editing the document

1 INTRODUCTION

1.1 Scope of the chapter

This chapter considers the series of operations which are carried out after the author has completed the document and up to its appearance in some published physical form.

Author and editor are not necessarily clear-cut distinct roles, and many authors undertake what might be called editorial processes in planning and organizing the style of their manuscripts or in following stipulations provided by conference organizers and journal publishers. Equally the dictionaries and handbooks recommended for authors are valuable to editors, and many of the style manuals noted in Chapter 1 include sections on editing documents.

As emphasized in Chapter 1, the first objective in both the preparation of a document and its editing is to ensure that the content of the writing is clear, and that there is no obstruction in the flow of communication between author and reader.

Sometimes all the editing that is required to ensure this smooth flow is the marking up of copy for the compositor/printer/keyboard operator: headings, paragraphs, consistency in layout. In other cases the editor's tasks are more wide-ranging and may be considered as guiding authors in both style and content.

The responsible editor, without needing to be an expert on

A Guide to Information Sources for the Production of Documents

every aspect of typographic design, paper endurance, the economics of publishing, or the latest computer printing technology, may at any time require to know something about all these matters and to have some ideas about available sources of information. Hence the notes and references given here.

1.2 Summary of the chapter

2 Discusses the tasks and responsibilities of the editor, and distinguishes between copy-editing and creative editing; and describes some of the administrative responsibilities that the editor may also undertake, more particularly when acting also as publisher.
3 Lists the elements that make up a publication, from front matter to end matter, and gives notes on some of the more important of these; and draws attention to the editorial care required to provide biographical and bibliographic details.
4 Describes some of the administrative tasks which may become the responsibility of the editor, such as legal deposit and copyright.
5 Considers the editor in relation to printer and publisher, with notes on printing technology, the book trade and marketing; and the basic requirements of proof reading and proof handling.
6 Discusses briefly how new printing technology and the use of word processors are changing publication production and are also affecting the stability of contents and creating new bibliographic problems; and looks at these from the point of view of the editor.

1.3 Categories of publications

Most editors are familiar with different types of publication and recognize easily the particular bibliographic and physical requirements in editing a document for publication as a book, an article in a journal, a newsletter or conference proceedings.

For bibliographic purposes within the library and information communities the various existing types of publication have been carefully identified, distinguished and defined, with special bibliographic terms used. This has been considered necessary because there is the need to identify and describe bibliographically the smallest item within the larger, and, alternatively, to describe all the contents of a larger item made up of a number of parts.

In the traditional library catalogues with bibliographic records prepared on catalogue cards the solution was to make a 'unit entry' and use that 'unit entry' as many times with varying headings as there were items within a whole for which bibliographic records were required. In library and information systems much thought and planning have gone into designing computer programs where bibliographic levels are defined so that records can be manipulated from smallest item in relation to largest, from item to item, and so that the largest item is shown as the sum of the smaller.

As guidance for editors looking at publications from the point of view of the bibliographic details required, the common bibliographic terms used for publications are described here.

Monograph   The most common category of publication, the 'book', defined as a publication containing text and/or illustrations in eye-readable form:

> *Single-volume monograph*: complete in one physical part
> *Multi-volume monograph*: complete or intended to be completed in a finite number of separate parts.

In this category are included publications produced for a variety of purposes and occasions, such as theses and dissertations, conference proceedings, but which are complete in themselves, whether in one or more volumes. It is presumed that a multi-volume monograph has been conceived as an entity, but is split into volumes because of physical size or because of difference in contents; for example, one volume of written text and a second volume of illustrations.

Monographic series This kind of series is made up of a group of monographs, related to each other usually by subject, which have been issued in succession, by the same publisher and in a uniform style with a collective title applying to the group as a whole; but with each monograph in the series having its own individual title, title page, and pagination as well as including within the publication the collective title of the group.

A further distinction is made between:

- a *finite series*, where the number of monographs which are going to appear in the series is known and stated prior to publication;
- an *occasional* or *open series*, where the number of monographs to be included in the series is not known and the series may carry on indefinitely.

The distinction between these two can become blurred and publishers may even be hopeful that their *finite* series could over a long period become *open*: for example, a series originally intended to be *finite*, limited to monographs of the works of English poets, could develop into a series of works of poets writing in English and become open-ended. It can also be difficult to distinguish between a *monographic finite series* and a *multi-volume monograph*, particularly when the various volumes of the monograph are issued over a period, and publishers and authors may have forgotten or not known what was the original publication plan.

Serial Serial is the generic term used for a publication in any medium which is issued in successive parts, usually having a numerical or chronological designation, and intended to be continued indefinitely. Serials include a wide range of publications such as:

- periodicals; journals; newspapers; bulletins; newsletters;
- annuals; yearbooks; directories; reports; calendars; reviews;
- transactions; proceedings; memoirs; regular publications of learned societies;
- monographic series (see above).

Component part For purposes of bibliographic access or identification a component part can only be described by including some identification of the whole to which it belongs. Examples are:

- an article in a journal;
- a chapter in a monograph.

Instead of component part, the term 'analytic' is sometimes used.

For administrative purposes these bibliographic entities are distinguished through the use of the two international standard numbering systems, the International Standard Book Number (ISBN) and the International Standard Serial Number (ISSN):

- *Monographs*, whether single or multi-volume, are allocated an ISBN, which identifies one title, or edition of a title, from one specific publisher, and is unique to that publisher; that is, different binding editions have differing ISBNs.
- *Serials*, of all the kinds identified above, are allocated an ISSN, which relates to the title of the serial, and each ISSN is inseparably linked with a standardized form of title called 'key title'.
- *Monographs* grouped together as a *series*, whether *finite* or *open*, are allocated an ISBN for each individual mono-

graph in the series, and will also bear the ISSN of the *series*.
- *Component parts*, which are articles in or parts of *serials*, may be cited in references by a short form which makes use of the ISSN of the serials (see 2.3.3).

The ISBN and the ISSN are also used in the library and information communities as bibliographic control numbers.

Some notes about the administrative aspects of the two numbering systems, from the point of view of the editor, are given in section 4 below.

2 CARRYING OUT EDITORIAL FUNCTIONS

An editor can anticipate carrying out a variety of functions and accepting to do these with varying degrees of responsibility. At one level, that of copy editor, the editorial role can be limited to dealing with manuscript and printer rather than author; at another level there are the tasks and responsibilities of substantive and creative editing.

The activities involved in copy editing should be relatively simple and straightforward: preparing a manuscript for publication by checking layout, spelling, style of headings; checking references and footnotes in accordance with agreed publishing style; marking up the copy for the printer; proof reading; copy correction.

Substantive and creative editing is undertaken by an editor who is expected to guide authors in the preparation of their manuscripts into a particular style and shape and to assist in the way in which their manuscripts have been planned and organized. An editor with this level of responsibility may be carrying out these functions for one particular journal; or for a series of publications in a specific subject range; or be preparing for publication papers first presented at a conference. Such an editor may carry the additional responsibilities of accepting contributions, but asking for changes or cuts; or of rejecting manuscripts on professional, ethical or even legal grounds. Editorial duties may extend to persuading authors to change, prune or rewrite texts, and the editorial relationship with any one author may be very personal, delicate and sensitive, a fine blend of demand, encouragement and persuasion. At the same time the editor may require a knowledge of copyright limitations and of possible legal complexities.

The editor carrying out substantive editing is likely in turn to be responsible to the editorial board of an institute or learned society, and editorial policy overall for the publications of the body will have been determined by the board. Editorial policy may also include decisions on marketing and publicity, and the editor may also be acting as publications officer and will be dealing with the administrative matters, such as keeping to legal deposit stipulations and preparing publicity brochures.

The majority of the editing manuals deal with all these kinds of editorial activities, and many also include information on some of the problems, both economic and administrative, in starting a newsletter or trying to distribute a report. Particularly useful are the editing guidelines directed at the problems of publishing in specific subject fields or directed at specialist audiences; for example, printing texts in mathematics or physics where special type faces are required; or publishing technical reports so that theory, experiment and conclusions are presented as a coherent whole. There are different traditions in different subject fields in presenting written text, particularly in relation to the layout and style of references, the introduction of quotations in the text or as footnotes, and the approach and appearance of an article in one of the social sciences may not be suitable for a scientific report.

Editorial style manuals The distinction between writing and editing, between author and editor, as already noted, is not necessarily clear-cut, and the style manuals listed in Chapter 1 generally include guidance on editorial tasks. There are also a wide range of editorial style manuals, some of which have been produced for a particular organization, publisher or learned society. Many of these refer to Fowler (32) and Gowers (34) as the basic source books.

One of the best known of the editorial style manuals, which is in use worldwide, is:

  The Chicago manual of style, 13th ed., rev., 1982 120

Other established handbooks are:

  Hart's rules for compositors and readers, 39th ed., 121
  1983

| Bodian | *Copywriter's handbook*, 1984 | 122 |
| Butcher | *Copy-editing*, 2nd ed., re., 1983 | 123 |

A comprehensive manual, with detailed instructions on typing layout, headings, capitalization, abbreviations, and so on, is that of the United Nations:

  United Nations *UN editorial manual*, 1983 87

A contrasting small but equally useful and more entertaining manual, with contents that are encyclopaedic as well as stylistic, has been produced by *The Economist* journal:

  The Economist pocket style book, 1986 124

Examples of other manuals prepared by organizations for their authors and editors are:

American Library Association	*Guidelines for authors, editors*, 1983	125
American Medical Association	*Style book and editorial manual*, 5th ed., 1971	126
Editerra editors' handbook, 1977		127
Modern Language Association of America	*Statement of editorial principles*, rev. ed., 1972	128

Manuals prepared specifically for special subjects can also be of more general use. One of the most valuable was sponsored by the International Federation of Scientific Editors' Association, the International Union of Biological Sciences, the International Union of Geological Sciences, and Editerra:

> O'Connor *Editing scientific books and journals*, 1978 129

and more recently there is the complementary text, which is more comprehensive than the title suggests:

> O'Connor *How to copyedit scientific books and journals*, 1986 130

Guidelines for editing special types of publications are provided in:

> Arnold *Editing the organizational publication*, 1982 131
> Bentley *Editing the company publication*, new ed., 1975 132
> Beach *Editing your newsletter*, 2nd ed., 1983 133
> Ferguson *Editing the small magazine*, 2nd ed., 1976 134
> Wales *A practical guide to newsletter editing and design*, 2nd ed., 1976 135
> DeBakey *The scientific journal: guidelines for editors, reviewers and authors*, 1976 136
> Swanson *Mathematics into type*, rev. ed., 1982 137

To assist the uniform presentation of scientific publications, Unesco has sponsored the preparation and production of specialized guidelines including:

Unesco	*Style manual for the presentation of English-language manuscripts intended for publication by Unesco*, 1981	138
Grünewald	*Guidelines for editing scientific and technical journals*, 1979	139
Martinsson	*Guide for the preparation of scientific papers for publication*, 2nd ed., 1983	140

3 MAKING UP THE PUBLICATION

In preparing a document for publication the editor attends not just to the manuscript which the author has provided but makes sure of the presence of the elements which are necessary for:

- biographical information;
- bibliographic identification;
- subject content description; and also
- physical completion.

Whatever type of publication is planned, some or all of the following elements will be required, normally in the order of:

Front matter
- cover and spine
- half-title (the title of the publication standing alone on a page)
- title page
- verso of the title page
- foreword
- preface (including, where relevant, acknowledgements)
- table of contents

- explanatory notes (including, where relevant, list of abbreviations and acronyms)
- abstract

Body of the text, including
- introduction
- substantive chapters
- conclusions and recommendations

End matter
- annexes
- appendices
- notes
- glossary
- bibliography or list of references
- index
- back cover

The general editorial manuals discuss all these elements, and there are some special manuals dealing with topics such as indexing and abstracting. Some international standards provide guidance on presentation including:

    ISO 8–1977   *Presentation of periodicals*, 1977   141

and:

    ISO 5966–1982; ISO 7144–1986; ISO 215–1986   54, 55, 57

and the British Standard equivalent:

    BS 2509–1970 (1983)   58

A guide produced by the Cambridge University Press in its series of authors' and printers' guides deals with the problems of both the beginning and end of a publication:

    Burbidge   *Prelims and end-pages*, 2nd ed., 1969   142

3.1 Front matter

Cover and spine The cover of a publication at its most simple and economical can repeat all or some of the elements of the title page; that is, be identical in the typography and layout but be produced on firmer paper or board. On the other hand, to arouse interest and promote sales, the publisher may choose to have the cover designed in such a way as to represent the contents or the purpose of the book. Practices vary according to country – in some countries the cover is considered as important a source of information as the title page – and the publisher, as well as the kind of publication and its intended market.

An international standard on the way in which spine titles should run has been agreed:

    ISO 6357–1985   *Spine titles on books and other publications*, 1985   143

and its British Standards equivalent:

    BS 6738–1986   *Recommendations for the presentation of spine titles*, 1986   144

Half-title and title page The title-leaves consisting of half-title and recto and verso of the title page are covered by an international standard now under revision:

    ISO/DP1086–1987   *Title-leaves of books*   145

which aims to help publishers and editors produce title-leaves in a form which will facilitate their use by bibliographers, librarians and researchers. The half-title, in addition to the title of the publication, can include a statement of a series with the number or designation of the publication within that series.

The most important elements on the title page are the title of the work and the name of the author of that work, and an editor may be involved with the author in discussing both title and form of name.

Both author and editor, when discussing a new title, are concerned that it should not be too long, too wordy, too vague, too technical, generic. Indeed the negative attributes of title-making are easily recognizable and more readily acknowledged than the positive: that wherever possible the title should be short, specific and descriptive, not dependent upon a lengthy subtitle to explain contents and scope. In many instances both author and editor are forced to recognize the limitations of title-making and accept a compromise (as for example with this work). But a good title is important, in promoting the use of a work and in its publicity and marketing. It can be the major tool for literature search in bibliographies and catalogues, in the abstracting and indexing services and in the current awareness lists.

With serials, generic titles, which indicate the type of publication and the subject – such as 'Journal of Physics', 'Library Science Bulletin', 'Information Newsletter' – lead to confusion, even with the addition of the name of a society or institution. Within the International Serials Data System (ISDS), which is responsible for the allocation of International Standard Serials Numbers (ISSN), a unique title for each serial registered, called a 'key title', is formulated, making use of its distinguishing features such as the institution, the place of publication and the dates of publication. An editor, when discussing possible titles for a new serial, might usefully consult an international directory of serials or the national ISDS centre, which is more usually located as a department of the national library (see also section 4 below).

The editor, when discussing with an author or group of authors, the forms in which names are to be presented on the title page (and thereafter in all literature and publicity about the publication) wants to make sure that biographical and bibliographic requirements are satisfied as well as personal preferences. There may well be a degree of sensitivity on the part of an author about parts of a personal name or professional qualifications or dates of birth; and this may well be offended if an agreed short form of name on the title page is obviated by the appearance of a full form with dates in a cataloguing-in-publication entry (see 4 below) on the back of the title page.

Group sensitivity can be even stronger and less easily assuaged when the publication has been produced by a number of authors, and there is a delicacy in agreeing a wording which exactly defines the extent of the contributions of each in the group. 'Compiled by ... with illustrations by ...' is a statement easily understood in its division of responsibility. More difficult to agree, and to distinguish, are statements such as 'in collaboration with', 'in association with', 'with contributory authors'. An editor may need much skill in identifying degrees of authorship, particularly in some academic works, and in persuading authors to agree a title page statement about their contributions.

There can also be problems when a corporate body, that is, an association, institution or even a governmental organization, has taken on the role of author or compiler, and is responsible for statements made or the conclusions presented. Alternatively responsibility may be shared between a personal author and a corporate body; for example, a conference may be sponsored by a learned society but the proceedings of that conference have been edited by an individual. An editor must ensure that the layout and wording of the title page reflect clearly, and where possible simply (though given the complexities of corporate body structure and hierarchy this is not always possible), distinctions in intellectual responsibility.

The verso of the title page is where the bibliographic details about the publication are more usually printed, and most publications will provide some or all of the following details:

- copyright information: see 2.4.2;
- the full address of the publisher;
- the International Standard Book Number (ISBN) of the publication; and possibly other ISBNs relating to previous editions of the work and other binding editions of the publication;
- when the publication is part of a monographic series, the International Standard Serial Number (ISSN) of the series: see 1.3 above;
- a Cataloguing-in-Publication (CIP) entry provided by the national CIP agency in cooperation with the publisher: see 4 below;
- descriptive details of printing and type face, and possibly name and address of printer.

In some countries there is a legal requirement to provide the full official name of the author on the verso of the title page.

Some types of publications lack the usual form of title-leaves, and bibliographic information may be found at the end of the publication in the colophon (traditional in some countries) or on the masthead of a serial or as part of the contents list. In library and bibliographic terms such sources of information are known as 'title page substitutes'.

Foreword and preface A foreword and a preface can appear together in a publication, with different purposes which are often confused. A foreword is an introductory statement written by someone other than the author. A preface, written by the author, sets out the origins, purpose and scope of the publication, and sometimes includes acknowledgements. Both are different from the introduction to the publication, which deals with the subject of the work.

Table of contents The international standard for contents lists of periodicals can also be followed for the contents of other types of publications:

| ISO 18–1981 | Contents list of periodicals, 1981 | 146 |

Explanatory notes; list of abbreviations and acronyms Author and editor may consider it useful, or essential, to provide explanatory notes before the body of the text. Such notes might be a disclaimer of responsibility about some aspect of the work, or an explanation on the usage of terms used in the text.

In some subject fields a list of abbreviations and acronyms is essential: see 1.3.1.3.

Abstracts The use of abstracts, a form of brief introduction, is particularly common for journal articles and conference papers, and authors are often asked to contribute their own informative summary to precede the text. In other cases the task of preparing abstracts for all the articles in a journal issue or volume of conference proceedings may become the responsibility of the editor.

With the growth of the secondary services providing information about international publications in the fields of science, technology and information science, there has been increased concerned about the quality and consistency of abstracts, about how they are formulated and presented. As a consequence international standards, manuals and guidelines on the art of abstracting have been prepared. The basic international standards are:

| ISO 214–1976 | Abstracts for publication and documentation | 147 |
| ISO 5122–1979 | Abstract sheets in serial publications | 148 |

Manuals and guidelines include:

| Borko | *Abstracting concepts and methods,* 1975 | 149 |

Cremmins	*The art of abstracting*, 1982	150
Maizell	*Abstracting scientific and technical literature*, 1979	151
Rowley	*Abstracting and indexing*, 1982	152

An example of guidelines prepared by one of the large abstracting and indexing services for use by its own editors is:

American Chemical Society	*Directions for abstractors and section editors of Chemical Abstracts Service*, 2nd ed., 1971	153

3.2 Body of the text

The content of the body of the text is to a large extent determined by subject matter and purpose of the publication; and also influenced by the personal inclination of an author.

The body of the text can, in the case of a study or a report, comprise an introduction and substantive chapters; in the cases of a journal or periodical, separate articles, each with its own introduction and substantive chapters. The proceedings of a conference or meeting are likely to conclude with a summing up and recommendations.

3.3 End matter

Annexes and appendices There is no very great difference between the usage of the above terms: an appendix is considered as a complementary part of a document, not completely essential to the main body of the text, such as a list of acronyms, statistical tables, examples; an annexe supplements a document. The *UN editorial manual* makes a particular distinction: matter added to the main body of a document should usually be identified as an annexe; matter added to an annexe is identified as an appendix.

Notes and references Notes can be footnotes, notes at the end of chapters, or end-notes. Footnotes can present typographical problems and chapter notes are difficult to consult; end-notes can be considered more economical and easier to use.

In some subject fields notes are used extensively to expand information, provide an alternative argument; or in other cases and in some subject fields may simply be a reference to a bibliographic source.

Similarly the 'list of references' may also contain some 'notes'. A distinction is made when the 'list of references' becomes a bibliography of sources consulted or alternatively 'suggestions for further reading', and is compiled in alphabetical order, not as used in the body of the text. The differences between notes and references and their construction is dealt with in the general editorial manuals and in:

  Burbidge   *Notes and references,* 1952   154

There are wide variations in the ways in which bibliographic references are presented which extend to the order of the elements which make up the references, and the choice of those elements, to names, punctuation and capitalization. Hence, in order to ensure consistency, editors and publishers establish and insist on the use of a 'house style'.

A newly revised international standard for bibliographic references has been published:

  ISO 690–1987   *Bibliographic references:*   155
            content, form and structure,
            1987

and also a standard for the formulation of a unique bibliographic identification of articles in serials, useful for references and in abstracts:

  ISO 9115–1987   *Bibliographic identification*   156
            (biblid) of contributions in
            serials and books, 1987

Indexes The preparation of the index to a publication may be undertaken by its author in consultation with editor or publisher; or vice versa; or by an independent indexing expert. The style of index, its detail and extent, will depend upon the nature of the publication and its intended readership.

As indexing is one of the specialist activities of the secondary services and can also be considered as a fundamental aspect of library and information science, many manuals and guidelines are available and international standards have been prepared.

The international standard:

    ISO 999–1975   *Index of a publication*, 1975   157

has as its aim to enable publishers and editors to produce indexes in a form that facilitates their use by bibliographers, researchers and librarians.

The British Standards equivalent is:

    BS 3700–1976 (1983) *Recommendations for the*   158
    preparation of indexes to
    books, periodicals, 1976

Manuals include:

Anderson	*Book indexing*, 1987	159
Knight	*Indexing, the art of*, 1983	160
Butcher	*Typescript, proofs and indexes*, 1980	161

and the theoretical aspects of indexing and its vocabulary are dealt with in:

Borko	*Indexing concepts and methods*, 1978	162

Back cover In some countries it is a legal requirement that the names of publisher and/or printer, with their full addresses, are given on the last page of the text or on the recto of the back cover; in addition, as in France, the legal deposit number and date of deposit (see 2.4.1). It is now common to find the ISBN incorporated in, or in addition to, a machine readable bar-code; and the price.

3.4 Other descriptive and bibliographic details

To improve the identification and to enhance the description of a particular publication, the editor may need to include further information about contents and potential use within the publication. As already noted, such information is usually located on the verso of the title page; another possibility is inclusion in a preface. Some examples of important additional information are:

- relating the publication to other publications or to other editions of the work: whether there has been an earlier edition, or an edition under another title;
- stating that the work contained in the publication is a translation and giving the title of the original work;
- giving biographical details about translator or editor when details about the author are given elsewhere in the publication;
- providing the typographical details of design and type face;
- giving the specified number of the publication in a limited edition.

4 ADMINISTRATIVE ASPECTS OF EDITING

The editor, in the process of preparing the manuscript for publication, may also carry out a series of administrative tasks in order to make sure that the publication in its final physical form is legally identified and bibliographically described in full. From the point of view of marketing the latter is particularly important. In larger publishing businesses these tasks will be carried out as a matter of routine by other staff, but in the small business or where editor is also publisher, they will be part of the editorial responsibilities.

The bibliographic details identified in 2.3.1 suggest that the editor may need to be in touch with:

- the national ISBN agency;
- the national ISDS centre allocating ISSNs;
- the national CIP agency.

For a small publishing business the marketing advantages of joining the international numbering schemes, the ISBN and ISSN, and a national CIP programme outweigh the organizational and clerical problems of inserting additional steps into the routine of script to print; and there is no charge.

International Standard Book Numbers (ISBN) The ISBN is a 10 digit number which identifies uniquely each title and edition of a title, the publisher, language and country of the publisher. It will be used by publishers and booksellers for stock control, book ordering, and within the information communities as a bibliographic control number and in catalogues and bibliographic data bases.

The small publisher can apply directly to the national ISBN agency, which may be a division of the national library or an office within the national publishers' association, for the number which will identify the business and thereafter for an individual number for each title. That unique number can then be used in all promotional literature about the publication, and will be printed in the publication, on the verso of the title page and possibly the back cover; it will appear as one element in the national bibliographic record of the publication and will be used to identify the record in the national bibliographic data base.

The ISBN system is based on the international standard:

ISO 3297–1984   *International Standard Serial*   164
                 Numbering, 3rd ed., 1984

and the system is coordinated worldwide by the International ISBN Agency with its offices in Berlin.

International Standard Serial Numbers (ISSN)   The ISSN is an 8 digit number which identifies uniquely a serial title. It is used by publishers of journals and subscription agencies for stock control and subscription ordering; and within the information communities as a control number, for identification in catalogues, in abstracting and indexing services, and in references. For these purposes the ISSN is not used by itself but is always associated with a formalized title called the 'key title' which is determined by the national serial centre.

The small publisher producing a new serial applies directly to the national centre, which is usually situated within the national library, and is given an ISSN and the 'key title' of the new serial. That number is then printed on each issue of the serial, usually on the top right hand corner of the front cover, and can be used in all listings of the serial. It will appear in the national bibliographic record of the serial and will be used in the national bibliographic data base.

The national serial centre is part of the worldwide system, which was set up to assist the bibliographic control of serials as a means to improve communication in science and technology, the International Serials Data System, with its International Centre in Paris. The technicalities of creating ISSN are based on the international standard:

ISO 3297–1984   *International Standard Serial*   164
                 Numbering, 3rd ed., 1984

The bibliographic record for each serial allocated an ISSN also appears in the ISDS Register (more than 400,000 titles at the end of 1987) which is used as the base for a number of international union catalogues of serials.

Cataloguing-in-Publication (CIP) CIP programmes are cooperative schemes of publishers and librarians, with the aim of providing an early bibliographic record of a new publication which is printed in the book and appears in issues of the national bibliography. The advantages are in book selection for librarians and marketing and publicity for publishers and booksellers. The record in the publication is very brief, relating to author and title, but that advance record in the national bibliographic data base – or, through international cooperative library schemes, in the data bases of other countries – can produce a valuable collection of early pre-publication orders. The CIP programmes of the United States and the United Kingdom, for example, together represent an enormous English language market.

To join the CIP programme the small publisher applies to the national CIP agency, which will be part of the national bibliographic agency which in turn is usually situated within the national library, and will receive and complete CIP forms about each new publication well in advance of its appearance; in return will be sent a short catalogue entry for insertion on the verso of the title page; that entry will then be published as a bibliographic record in the national bibliography and/or in the bibliographic data base.

CIP programmes are nationally organized and differ in so far as publishing and publishers have different traditions. But library organizations have been concerned to establish international standards for their operations and for the entries that appear in the books. In these days of multinational or transnational publishing houses, for example, it is possible for a publication to be listed in two or three national data bases and hence have two or three CIP entries on the title page verso. There are publications with American, British and German CIP entries cluttering up the title page verso and causing much embarrassment throughout the international library world by their slight but significant differences.

To bring about some uniformity in approach, international

guidelines have been prepared and published by Unesco:

    Anderson   *Guidelines for cataloguing-in-*   165
                               publication, 1986

The three schemes are important to the small publisher by providing means of identification worldwide and bibliographic records that are used internationally and relate to worldwide markets. It is worth reiterating that there is no charge to the publisher to use an ISBN, an ISSN or CIP entry.

4.1 Legal deposit requirements

In a small publishing business editorial responsibility may extend to checking that the stipulated number of copies of the publication are deposited on publication at the office of legal deposit. This may be situated within the national library or as a separate office. There are considerable variations from country to country in the legal stipulations, varying in the number of copies demanded which can be as low as two or as high as eight, and the time allowance given to make the deposit, and the penalties for non-deposit. Each national legal deposit office will provide information about requirements and certificates of deposit. The publications deposited usually serve as the basis of the bibliographic records made for issues of the national bibliography.

    Legal deposit has been the source of innumerable long-term problems at both the national and international level, and endeavours have been made to reach international agreements which could then serve as the basis for international recommendations. To this purpose a study was undertaken and published by Unesco:

    Lunn   *Guidelines for legal deposit*,   166
                              1981

which has served as the working document in a number of countries where outdated laws of deposit are being redrafted.

There are still a few countries where there is no legal deposit but where it is usual for some scheme of voluntary deposit to function, as the collective responsibility of the publishers.

In some countries legal deposit is linked with the ISBN system and the allocation of ISBNs which thus become legal deposit numbers; this is the case in Spain. In other countries, as in France, the legal deposit number with date of deposit is printed in the publication, on the colophon or on the back cover.

4.2 Copyright requirements

The editor, without having a detailed knowledge of the intricacies of copyright law, should be aware generally of stipulations and problems and may need to:

- establish whether the copyright of the publication rests with the author (which is usual with a monograph and a single author); or if not, with whom; or if not a person, with what body;
- make sure that if extensive quotations are included in the text, or if illustrative material is being reproduced for inclusion in the text, formal requests for permission to reproduce quotations and illustrations have been sent to the copyright owners; and that acknowledgements of permission requested or granted are stated in the publication, in preface, colophon or captions.

Within the publication the statement of copyright and the name of the holder is usually set out on the verso of the title page, made up of the copyright symbol (a c in a circle), date of copyright and name of holder.

Some publishers waive copyright and state this clearly on the verso of the title page. Others reinforce the symbol with an additional statement claiming all rights reserved and that no part of the publication may be reproduced without permission in writing from the publishers. Because of these varying practices it is as well that the editor is scrupulous in applying for copyright permission whenever quotations or illustrations are being reproduced.

As guidance through the legal and linguistic complexities of copyright, Unesco published a 'copyright primer':

  Unesco   *The ABC of copyright*, 1981   167

which aims to provide practical answers to copyright questions expressed in non-legal easy-to-follow language.

Publications which deal with copyright internationally, within the European Community, in developing countries and in the United Kingdom, include:

Cavendish	*A handbook of copyright in British publishing practice*, 2nd ed. rev., 1984	168
Davies	*Challenge to copyright and related rights in the European Community*, 1983	169
DeFreitas	*The copyright system: practice and problems in developing countries*, 1983	170
Stewart	*International copyright and neighbouring rights*, 1983	171
Weil	*Modern copyright fundamentals*, 1985	172

5 THE EDITOR AND THE PUBLISHER AND PRINTER

All editorial activities are directed at the ultimate aim, to see the manuscript appear as a physical publication. In the processes leading to this, the editor may be consulting directly with publisher and printer; or may be taking on responsibilities of the three roles, in which case it will be necessary to have at hand expert reliable technical advice.

Every editor wants to create a good and attractive product and to be able to understand and appreciate the qualities of elegant type and clear layout. Without knowing all the details of modern printing technology, the editor needs to recognize the processes in relation to decisions on print run, paper weight and overall costs. The particular editorial expertise in proofreading implies an equal skill in the quick return of accurately corrected proofs.

A wide range of manuals and textbooks on every aspect of the printing industry are available, and international standards relating to printing are prepared by ISO/TC130, Graphic technology. A small selection of reference works and manuals is listed here.

5.1 Printing technology and typographic design

There are a number of attractive well illustrated introductory handbooks including:

Munce	*Graphics handbook*, 1982	173
Lewis	*Twentieth century book*, 2nd rev. ed., 1984	174

A useful small dictionary of English language publishing terms is:

Jacob	*A pocket dictionary of publishing terms*, 1976	175

Two multilingual dictionaries are:

Orne	*The language of the foreign book trade*, 3rd ed., 1976	176
Isaacs	*The multilingual dictionary of printing and publishing*, 1981	177

A five volume manual, prepared in the United Kingdom under the auspices of the National Council for the Training of Journalists, concentrates on newspaper design and typography but is very comprehensive:

Evan	*Editing and design*, 2nd ed., 1973–78	178

A standard work on book design, first published in 1956, brought up to date and revised, is:

Williamson	*Methods of book design*, 3rd ed., 1983	179

Two publications dealing with modern printing technology are:

Seybold	*Fundamentals of modern photocomposition*, 1979	180
Seybold.	*World of digital typesetting*, 1984	181

There is further discussion on printing technology in Chapter 3.

5.2 Publishing and the book trade

Guides addressed at the publishers of specialized texts and limited markets include:

Bodian	*Book marketing handbook*, 2 v., 1980–83	182
Day	*How to write and publish a scientific paper*, 2nd ed., 1983	183
Powell	*Getting into print: the decision-making process in scholarly publishing*, 1985	184
Smith	*Marketing for small publishers*, 1980	185

The publications noted in 1.3.6 are also relevant (105–110).

5.3 Proof reading and correction

Guidance on the handling of proofs can be found in the editorial style manuals: for example, the chapter in:

> O'Connor   *Editing scientific books and*   129
> *journals*, 1978

National standards for proof correction marks are carefully followed, but these standards differ, and as a consequence the practices of proof correction are very different and even contradictory in the marks used. For example, the practice in Central Europe differs from that in Western Europe which differs from that followed in the United Kingdom which differs from that followed in the United States.

It is not surprising that efforts are being made to draft an international standard for proof correction marks and usage, and this is being undertaken by ISO/TC130, Graphic Technology, in cooperation with ISO/TC46, Documentation. The British Standard includes recommendations for the preparation of copy as well as the correction of proofs:

> BS 5261–1975–6   *Guide to copy preparation*   186
> *and proof corrections*, 2 parts,
> 1975–76

As more and more authors are using word processors, the old practices of proof handling and correction are changing. This is discussed below at 2.6 and also in Chapter 3.

6 THE CHANGING ROLE OF THE EDITOR

As already noted, editors expect to undertake a variety of tasks with varying degrees of responsibility. In some ways, however, editing is still considered as an intellectual activity, something of a minor writing craft, in which skills of word usage, understanding of subject and style, of readers' needs, authors' limitations, all play a part: and at the same time the editor is expected to have a measure of technical practical knowledge.

The changes and rapid developments in information technology of the past decade have affected every aspect of printing and publishing including editing. Chapter 3 discusses some of the practical consequences of the new information technology, but here, as background, other consequences as they affect manuscript and editor are considered briefly. The points made here have already been explored in depth at conferences and seminars; for example, at the beginning of the 1980s in:

Hills	*The future of the printed word*, 1981	187

and in more recent publications including:

Gibson	*Editing in the electronic era*, 2nd ed., 1984	188
Gurnsey	*The information professions in the electronic age*, 1985	189

Many of the new forms of printing and publishing – for example, the use of computer-based text processing systems and printing by photocomposition – although they differ from the traditional in that they are quicker and streamline various operations, produce publications that are not so very different from those produced by traditional technology: they are still books, paper-based, hand-holding, eye-readable. But the new processes mean that some of the old stages in book production can be omitted; for example, galley proofs, page proofs. Hence the need for author and editor to pay even closer attention to consistency and high standards in the preparation of manuscripts. Authors' traditional bad habits of making amendments and updating at proof stage can no longer be acceptable.

A more fundamental result of the new forms of technology has been the change in the relationship between the intellectual 'work' contained in the physical product the 'book'; and as a consequence new ideas about publishing.

Books are now dealt with in much the same way as any other marketable product, subject to extensive advertising and marketing campaigns, with retail sale outlets everywhere – in supermarkets and drugstores. At the other extreme is the practice of 'demand' publishing, adopted for some specialist scientific journals, where the text is reproduced only when requested and paid for. A new style of bibliographic problem is presented by the publication on tape or disc which is in a constant state of change as the author amends, adjusts, improves.

The new attitude, that publications become out of date rapidly and are therefore expendable, is influencing the role of the information community with queries asked about its purpose and responsibilities and how expensive information services can continue to exist when the products they provide are easily available or rapidly superseded.

There is an increasingly wide range of new 'information products', such as machine readable files, video discs, microforms, and there have been discussions about the future 'paperless society' when all the products of information are packaged in forms other than books.

But the paper-based products, the books and the journals, still predominate worldwide, and are likely to do so, because their advantages in human terms outweigh any others that machines can offer. There will continue to be economic conditions when machines will not be available and environmental circumstances where to use a machine would be a barrier to understanding and a handicap to the reader.

Whatever the packaging and in whatever form information is prepared for presentation to the reader, the information itself must be organized and arranged in such a way that it is intelligible and of use to the reader. From this point of view it would seem that there will be a continuing role for editors in preparing documents for publication; but they may require a higher degree of technical knowledge and skills.

3

Producing and publishing the document

1 INTRODUCTION

1.1 Scope of the chapter

Preparing the document for publication in terms of how the text is set out and marked up has been looked at in Chapters 1 and 2. This chapter starts by taking the preparation of the document a stage further and looks at the ways in which author and editor prepare a text by typewriter or by word processor. At this stage the physical form of the end product, whether it is to appear as a monograph, journal article, in hard copy or in microform, does not influence the author's task.

On the other hand it is at this stage that there can now be the most intimate relationship between author and the published text. As already discussed in Chapters 1 and 2, the introduction of the new information technology, of electronic processing and computer-based equipment, has brought about some remarkable changes in the ways in which documents can be produced. Many of the old requirements for composition and compositors have disappeared, and authors may be preparing a text on a typewriter in 'camera ready' form or may be inputting text directly on to tape or disc which will then be phototypeset.

Word processors are a relatively new form of equipment, are in use worldwide dependent upon certain environmental conditions, are developing fast and becoming easier to use as microcomputers become more capable and more economical. In such a changing environment it is not possible to list standards and recommended equipment, but instead suggestions are made about what to look for in a word processor and the problems that can arise. Many authors and editors, in using a word processor, find that they need, or wish, to know something more of the background of computer technology, computer terminology, and of the standards that are in use throughout the computer industry. A brief introduction is provided listing some dictionaries, manuals, reference books and journals, with an account of the work of the international standardizing bodies.

In the remainder of the chapter the various physical forms of publication are looked at from the point of view of author and editor who may require to know about technical aspects of printing or microfilming without necessarily being involved in highly detailed manufacturers' specifications.

For the purposes of the chapter the definitions of 'to produce', 'production', 'to publish' and 'publication' are taken from the *Oxford Reference Dictionary* (28):

- 'to bring before the public'
- 'to manufacture from raw materials'
- 'to bring into existence'
- 'being produced or manufactured, especially in large quantities'
- 'a thing produced, especially a literary or artistic work'
- 'to issue copies of (a book or periodical, newspaper, etc.) for sale to the public'
- 'the issuing of a book or periodical etc. to the public'
- 'a book etc. so issued'

1.2 Summary of the chapter

2 Discusses the ways in which the manuscript is prepared for publication making use of a typewriter or word processor;

gives some background about word processors and computers and of how author and editor are now directly involved in publishing; notes some of the international standardizing bodies in the field of information technology.
3 Describes the various processes involved in producing documents in paper-based form, as books, journals, etc.; and discusses the design of the publication, paper, composition and printing, binding.
4 Discusses the use of microform in producing documents; considers how best microforms can be used.
5 Considers the multimedia publication, where one part consists of a paper-based brochure and other parts are audio-visual aids dependent upon special equipment.

2 PREPARING THE TEXT FOR PUBLICATION

2.1 From typewriter to word processor

Today the majority of authors, in preparing their texts for publication, will use, or will have access to, some kind of typewriter and will produce texts which are easy to read and which have been set out according to author's wishes or editor's instructions. The style manuals listed in Chapters 1 and 2 include instructions on how the manuscript can be converted into typed pages, and some manuals give very detailed rules on spacing, underlining, indentation of paragraphs, etc. These recommendations vary according to the manuals, but basically all are variations of standard and limited proposals, in much the same way as the layout possible on the conventional typewriter is standard and limited.

Until recently the typewriter keyboard could offer only upper and lower case letters and a limited range of additional keys. On the other hand the range of typewriters is enormous, in size, weight and price, whether designed for heavy duty in an office or for the business traveller or for home use. But whatever the kind and the manufacturer, all typewriters – and all typists when moving from one machine to another – have benefited from having the same keyboard, in the roman script and in other scripts; keyboards established in accordance with ISO standards.

The universal use of the 'QWERTY' roman alphabet keyboard has continued as typewriters have become electric and then electronic. Electric typewriters help typists' speeds, but do not extend the operations which the machines can perform. It was the development of automatic and electronic typewriters with memories and the interchange of type face which brought about new possibilities for typists and typed pages. These in turn have led on to the electronic display typewriters, or video typewriters, comprising display screens and internal memories as well as keyboards. In many offices the next stage has been to upgrade electronic typewriters to word processors; or alternatively, to change from typewriters to word processors.

The development of word processors came about as an application of general-purpose computers to the particular functions of text preparation and editing. As computer technology became less expensive word processors were designed specifically for office use and for writing and editing, and in many cases those using word processors were not consciously aware that they were now involved with computers.

The development of microcomputers has since increased the range of word processors and their capabilities. At one end of the market there are now available word processors complete with keyboard, visual display screen and printer, which are not very much more expensive than the electronic typewriter; and there are others, designed to be used in offices or as part of a network, which are more complex, capable of many more functions and very much more expensive. It is an expanding and changing market with a continuous stream of new products, both the hardware, the machines, and the software, the programs for the machines.

2.2 Making use of a word processor

With the conventional typewriter, whether manual or electric, standard or portable, there is no distinction between the preparation of the text and its appearance: that is, the letter key is struck and that letter appears immediately on the printed page. With word processors making use of keyboard and visual display screen, the preparation of the text and its final printed presentation are logically two separate processes. Some of the facilities which the word processor provides, which are additional to any that can be found in the traditional typewriter, are:

- frequently used page settings can be stored and generated with a few key strokes to give margins, tab settings, page lengths, etc.;
- frequently used phrases can be stored and generated by a short sequence of key strokes;
- standard paragraphs can be stored for use with appropriate introductory phrases and final greetings;
- corrections to spelling of words can be made using the cursor, and adjustments to the text are made by the computer;
- 'cut/paste' operations in the preparation of drafts, reports, etc., are made easier.

The software packages designed to streamline the writing and editing functions of word processors incorporate the features noted above, and usually many more. Producing the text physically from the word processor depends upon its printer, with the encouraging possibilities of desk top publishing (DTP): see 3.3.4.

An author changing from the conventional typewriter, with the consequent strain of the manual operations of rewriting, cutting and pasting, retyping and copying, can find that using a word processor brings new dimensions to text preparation: productivity as a typist is improved and the final typed product is enhanced; more importantly, a different style of authorship becomes possible. There is the mental relief in knowing that drastic revision of text will no longer mean substantial retyping and that the abandoned paragraph or unconnected section will not be lost but can be stored for re-examination later and integration in the text at the correct place.

In the office the productivity gains may be such as to release staff for other duties. Moreover word processors, by making correction and amendment of text relatively easy and by ensuring virtually a consistent high quality of output, can be used directly by staff with no formal training as typists. It is soon possible to become a proficient 'two finger typist' and find using the word processor in this way is preferable to writing reports in longhand for later transcription by the regular typists.

Word processors are in the forefront of the technological changes involved in bringing automation into the office and into all professions and industries connected with text production, presentation and publication. Wherever introduced they are likely to produce changes in working practices, in individual responsibilities, and personnel relationships no less dramatic and drastic than followed the advent of automation in industry generally. One of the best recorded examples has been the change within the newspaper industry, where the introduction of new techniques has brought about what is known as a 'revolution'. The long established distinctions between the editorial and advertising departments and the composition and reprographic departments have broken down. It is now the responsibility of the editorial and advertising staff to input and assemble all the text and illustrative elements directly on to pages ready for printing. For a member of the editorial staff information processing means replacing the typewriter with the word processor with its facilities to write and edit copy which can then go straight to producing the galleys of text for pasting up the pages.

In Chapter 1, section 1.3.5 some introductory reports on how the use of word processors is changing the ways of authors and editors are listed. This is a literature field that is changing and expanding as rapidly as the machines and their new facilities. Many manuals, of course, are written specifically for particular machines or programs, but some more general introductions to word processors have appeared, including:

Derrick	*The word processing handbook*, 1984	190
Wells	*Low-cost word processing*, 1986	191

A specialist application for a profession which has long been burdened with problems of standard paragraphs, drafting and retyping, is:

Townsend	*Word processing for solicitors*, 1983	192

There is the possibility of keeping up to date through issues of a specialist periodical such as:

The international word processing report, 1979–   193

A manual which deals with the whole subject of the design and layout of the printed page, whether the text is produced on paper or on screen, is:

Jonassen	*The technology of text*, 1982	194

Among the very specialist multilingual dictionaries there is:

Vollnhals	*Elsevier's dictionary of word processing (English, French, German)*, 1986	195

2.3 Background to computers, word processors and electronic publishing

Many authors, in learning to use a word processor, come to accept that they are now using a computer and find they need, or wish, to know something of the background of computing, computer terminology, and of the possibilities of their machines and their potential for adaptation and expansion.

A wide range of dictionaries and reference manuals dealing with various aspects of computers and computing applications is available, is developing and changing. In this field of information technology, there is the necessity that such manuals are continuously updated and revised in order to reflect advances in the technology and changes in the terminology.

Dictionaries and encyclopedias which provide an introduction to computers include:

Illingworth	*Minidictionary of computing*, 1986	196
Longley	*Macmillan dictionary of information technology*, 2nd ed., 1986	197
Meadows	*Dictionary of computing and information technology*, 3rd ed., 1987	198
Sippl	*Macmillan dictionary of microcomputing*, 3rd ed., 1985	199
Stokes	*Concise encyclopedia of information technology*, 3rd ed., 1986	200

As is apparent in the above list, publishers are appreciative of the need to produce revised updated editions very frequently; and some of those noted above may have already been replaced with later versions.

Producing and Publishing the Document

Even more useful are the year books and reference handbooks which cover every aspect of computers and computing, equipment, applications, personnel and even salaries, and which are extensively revised each year. Because computing technology is a new and international field of science, these reference books produced in the English language have international applicability; an example is:

    The computer users' year book, 4 v., 1988   201

which includes sections on services, standards, salary survey.

    Deighton   *Computers and information*   202
                             processing world index, 1984

covers a similar range of topics, lists national and international standardizing bodies and 800 journals in the subject field which are published worldwide.

As the market of microcomputers and word processors has widened, it has become increasingly difficult to know how to choose equipment or system. There is the possibility of consulting a computer service agency; or of making use of a guide such as:

    Longley   *The microcomputer user's*   203
                             handbook, 1985

Another way is to watch over the journals produced in the field, the majority of which include a survey of new models and of prices. Some of the journals of international applicability are:

    Information media and technology   204

which is the journal of the National Centre for Information Media and Technology (Cimtech) in the United Kingdom, and which surveys new equipment and undertakes evaluation reports.

    International journal of micrographics and video   205
    technology

covers all aspects of electronic information transfer and was formerly published under the titles *Microdoc* and *Micropublishing of current periodicals*.

    Microcomputers for information management   206

is an international quarterly journal addressed specifically at library and information services.

    Information processing and management   207

which incorporates *Information technology* is more concerned with basic and applied research in information and communication studies.

    There are also an increasing number of works looking at the wider implications of office automation and electronic publishing (see also 2.6 and 3.3.4). The National Computing Centre (NCC) in the United Kingdom has published:

| Condon | *Text creation in the electronic office*, 1983 | 208 |

The problems of technology in relation to copyright, consumer demand etc., are examined in:

| Greenberger | *Electronic publishing plus*, 1985 | 209 |

Finally, when the English language terms are insufficient for international communication, there are the multilingual dictionaries, such as:

| Nania | *Complete multilingual dictionary of computer terminology (English, French, Italian, Portuguese)*, 1984 | 210 |

2.4 Standards for computers and computing applications

From the beginning, because of its newness and international applications, the development of international standards in the field of computers and computing applications has been considered important, not just to the manufacturers, but also more significantly to the purchasers of equipment and the users, by helping to ensure compatibility and hence the possible interchange among equipment and products; this by reducing the user's dependence upon one type of equipment and possibly one source of supplies.

At the moment there are some 700 international standards and draft standards covering every aspect of computer hardware, software applications, and dealing with other matters such as safety, ergonomic factors in design, personnel needs. These standards can be grouped under the following topics:

- guides or codes of practice designed to raise the level of computing work generally;
- specifications for equipment and operational procedures, which will permit the interchangeability of equipment or the interchange of data;
- specifications to establish the quality of the consumable goods used in computer applications, such as discs, tapes;
- application standards, prepared by groups of users with a common interest; for example, for applications in banking, data interchange, preparation of bibliographic records;
- standards that form a generally agreed basis for the interconnection or interworking of many items of equipment of different manufacture;
- standard programming languages, which assist the application programs to be moved from one processor to another, thus protecting the user's investment in software.

In addition to ISO there are other organizations involved in the development of international standards in computing and electronic engineering, including:

- International Electrotechnical Commission (IEC), which

is the primary international authority in developing standards on electrical equipment including computers and office equipment;
- the Consultative Committee of the International Telecommunications Union (CCITT), which has primary responsibility for standards affecting the telecommunications process, and which works closely with ISO on all user aspects of data transmission standards;
- European Computer Manufacturers' Association (ECMA), which has been responsible for the technical content of many recent computer standards. ECMA works closely with ISO and prepares some drafts which then go to ISO. It has also established a close liaison with American computer groups, and its standards, which are free, can be considered to have international applicability.

The standards produced by ECMA are in essence a set of harmonized approved and authoritative guidelines for system designers, leaving a measure of choice with options and alternatives. As a guide to the use of its standards, ECMA has produced its own interpretation of what standards are and how they should be applied:

    ECMA   *The meaning of conformance*   211
                       to standards, 1983

which concludes with a set of precise recommendations on use. An example of an ECMA standard prepared in association with IEC in a non-technical area is:

    ECMA   *Safety requirements for data*   212
                       processing equipment, 2nd
                       ed., 1981

Another type of ECMA standard is:

    ECMA   *Ergonomics –*   213
                       recommendations for VDU
                       work places, 1984

Because computers and computing applications have a high international element the majority of the standards developed by national bodies are linked to or correspond closely with the international standards developed by the bodies noted above.

In the continuing and expanding work on standards, these international organizations, in consultation with manufacturers and national and international user groups, are involved in the preparation of new standards as need is shown. Currently work is under way in examining the need for standards in the specific areas of:

- open systems interconnection, whereby computer systems or terminals can interwork in a general or open way, based on the use of standards rather than requiring individual negotiations between systems;
- local area networks, which allow personal computers, word processors, terminals etc., to be linked together in one location;
- text communication, covering the preparation, processing, and interchange of text in documents;
- data transmission;
- computer graphics;
- programming language compiler validation, to improve the portability of programs between different computers;
- quality assurance, to improve the quality of the manufactured computer products; manufacturers can register as producing equipment or products of assessed quality.

3 PRODUCING DOCUMENTS ON PAPER

The rapid advances in information technology, which have made it possible to consider reproducing texts in different physical forms, have also made it possible to produce the traditional paper-based publications – books, journals, newspapers – faster and cheaper. The advantages of these kinds of publication for readers – that they can be held in the hand, require no extra equipment, can be read anywhere at any time – far outweigh their disadvantages, which are more apparent to publishers, indexing services and librarians, of bulk in storage, weight in despatch, and possibly a short lifespan. Generally the first choice of editor and author, when considering the document as a published product, is likely to be text on paper.

In Chapter 2.5, it is suggested that editors and authors, while not requiring to be experts in every aspect of the printing industry, may wish to know something about its technology, and some background texts and manuals are listed. Technical matters are considered in more detail in this section, including the totality of desk top publishing.

3.1 Designing the publication

A well designed book or serial has a unified appearance throughout, with all the chapters or articles set out in the same style, and with cover, front and end matter consistent with that style. Achieving this appearance of typography and layout comes as the result of discussion between the editor and the printer with the print designer.

The final agreed print specifications will be a balance between appearance and costs, and the final product should relate to the content of the document, its intended readership, and anticipated lifespan.

The detailed printing specifications should be agreed between editor and publisher or printer at an early stage in discussions on the publication, and should include all or some of the following points:

- size of the page;
- quality and weight of the paper;
- approximate number of pages in the monograph; or in each issue of a serial;
- type founts for all parts of the publication, including front

matter, running heads, references, headings, tables, etc.;
- type size and body for the different parts;
- type area or imposition size; that is, the length of the lines and the number of lines on each page;
- style and arrangement of the headings and legends to go with tables, columns, illustrations;
- style for reference lists and bibliographies;
- style for indexes;
- placement of page numbers;
- symbols to be used to identify footnotes or references.

Once these specifications have been agreed, specimen pages can be prepared showing all the details, and from these a style sheet can be made up from which the typescript will be marked up for the compositor or keyboarder.

3.2 Choosing the paper

The editor in discussing the physical appearance of the publication with printer and designer may wish to take into account some aspects of the paper on which the publication is to be printed: for example:

- weight of the paper: in relation to the size of the publication; whether as a serial it will be despatched by mail and hence a lightweight paper is an advantage;
- texture and finish: in relation to the print and illustrations;
- durability: is the publication ephemeral to be replaced by another edition in a short time; will the paper deteriorate when stored;
- thickness in relation to boards for the cover and the type of binding to be used.

International standards exist for the manufacture of paper and boards, prepared by ISO/TC 6, Paper, board and pulps, with ISO/TC 130, Graphic technology, and these cover all the above points and also specific matters such as the opacity of paper, its bursting strength, roughness, absorption of water or oil. The editor may also want to know how to estimate quantities and costs and some guidance is provided by manufacturers' handbooks such as:

 Alder   *The bookman's book*, 1969 214

An international standard for paper sizes was agreed as long ago as 1975 and covers the A and B series:

 ISO 216–1975   *Writing paper and certain* 215
         classes of printed matter, 1975

with the British Standard equivalent included in:

 BS 4000–1983   *Specification for size of paper* 216
         and board, 1983

Size A4, recommended for typescripts, correspondence, etc., is used for monographs and serials; A5 (half of A4) is considered suitable for pamphlets; A6 (half of A5) is designed for postcards. These sizes are in use worldwide, but are not used in some countries, such as the USA, and as a consequence there can be problems in reprographic copying and printing.

3.3 Putting the text on to paper: composition

The basic process of 'printing' is made up of two main operations, the first that of composition (typesetting or keyboarding), followed by the actual printing (the presswork or machining).

The main methods of composition, going from the traditional to the new techniques, are:

- handsetting, which is used as little as possible today as it is slow and expensive; but it may be required for special settings, for complex tables, mathematical equations or chemical formulae;
- 'hot-metal' or 'hot-lead' composition on Linotype, Monotype, or similar machines: with Linotype whole lines

Producing and Publishing the Document

of type are cast from a reservoir of molten metal after the compositor has keyboarded the copy: Monotype machines produce single characters from a similar hot-metal alloy; the keyboards on both types of composing machines look like large typewriters;
- 'camera-ready copy', which can be prepared on any typewriter or word processor, consists of a typescript which has been carefully prepared ready for printing by offset lithography or by photocomposition: the advantages are in the economy of production and speed and the elimination of proof reading; the disadvantages are that typed characters take up more space than typeset characters and that the appearance of the typed page is not as attractive as the typeset page;
- computer-assisted photocomposition, using electronic and photographic methods; from the keyboard images of type characters are projected from a film or disc on to photo-sensitive film or paper which is used to produce an offset plate; there are differences among the machines and continuing changes and developments; some produce magnetic tape, others cassettes or floppy discs; some have a visual display screen on which the keying process can be seen complete with coded instructions as well as a visual representation of how the final text will appear; the advantages of photocomposition are speed, the flexibility of type size and form, and the help in consistency and layout provided by the computer;
- making use of word processors: see 3.2.2.

The rapid developments of the past decade in printing technology have meant that the literature on the subject is not all up to date. Brochures produced by manufacturers are helpful and also the journals and year books produced by or for the printing industry. Two old established books produced by bookmen which deal with traditional methods leading on to the new are:

A Guide to Information Sources for the Production of Documents

    Morison   *First principles of typography*, 217
                                2nd ed., 1967
    Jennett   *The making of books*, 5th ed., 218
                                1973

See also the publications listed in Chapter 2.5, 2.6, and Chapter 1.3.6.

A comprehensive guide to every aspect of the printing industry which is kept up to date on a yearly basis is produced in the United Kingdom by the British Printing Industries Federation:

    BPIF   *Printers' yearbook*, 1985/86   219

which includes a glossary, sections on industrial relations and law, and the standards recommended from inks to microfiche.

The keyboarding stage in composition can be eliminated when the original manuscript or typescript can be 'read' by scanning using optical character recognition (OCR) equipment. At first there was a limitation to the type founts which such machines could follow, but recently there have been new developments of intelligent character recognition (ICR) which means that an unlimited variety of typefaces and even handwriting can be handled by the scanning machines. The scanners produce paper or magnetic tape for photocomposition or can be linked directly.

OCR makes possible input directly from typewriter to phototypesetting or from typewriter to word processors. Of particular interest to librarians and archivists are possible applications in 'reading' a variety of older records and hence of updating bibliographies and catalogues; for example, catalogue cards produced over a long period and in a variety of styles can be 'read' and then printed out in a consistent style. Some experience in the use of OCR in information services and libraries is set out in:

    Smith   *Optical character recognition*, 220
                                1985

3.4 Printing the document

The traditional printing processes are:

- letterpress, which is used mainly in conjunction with 'hot-metal' composition;
- offset lithography, in which the film produced by the composition process is photographically reproduced on printing plates.

Recent developments following upon computer-aided photo-composition have introduced new ways in which the plates are made, or alternatives to making plates; for example, in laser printing a laser beam creates character images on to a photosensitive belt or drum, which are developed and transferred to paper. The old established manufacturers of 'hot-metal' printing machines, Linotype and Monotype, are now producing a wide range of sophisticated and laser typesetters.

'In-house' printing Associated with the use in offices and homes of microcomputers and word processors (see 3.2.2) is the growing interest in setting up 'in-house' printing operations which will be economical in time and effort and will produce attractive internal brochures, documents, newsletters, etc. In organizations where a large-scale sophisticated copying machine is already installed for other functions, reproduction 'in-house' can be even more economical.

Choosing a printer for office or home use depends on the volume of the intended use, special printing needs, and the operating environment (that is, printers can be noisy). When the printer is purchased as a separate item, the first and major consideration is that of compatibility. Printers must not be considered in isolation but as part of a total system, and must be compatible in terms of hardware, software and general operating requirements. The best way to ensure compatibility is to see the total system in operation: there are too many sad tales of important texts being put on to floppy discs which cannot be used on the available printer.

Some of the features to consider in making the choice are:

- print method: daisywheel where the print looks as though it came from a typewriter, available with a wide range of different type styles and foreign language alphabets; dot matrix, where the quality of the printing is not as good, but is faster and cheaper;
- justified margins: a right-hand justified margin improves the appearance of the page;
- underlining and bold print: not available in all printers;
- maximum paper width;
- types of paper which can be used with the printer;
- maximum print speed;
- the interface standard for connecting the printer to the computer.

Surveys of printers are given, with those of other equipment, in the journals and year books; for example, there is an up to date and comprehensive survey of computer printers in:

    Deighton   *Computers and information*   202
                                  processing world index, 1984

An evaluation guide prepared by the National Computing Centre in the United Kingdom is:

    Condon   *Office printers*, 1982   221

The printer and the printing operation can be just part of a total system of desk top publishing.

Desk top publishing (DTP) In the publishing industry the advent of DTP, which has already acquired the particular status of capitals and initials, promises to be a revolution as fundamental as was the shift to direct input by journalists; and its potential for the small association publisher, or the editor/publisher, or the 'do-it-yourself' author/publisher, is impressive.

At its most simple, DTP is a more sophisticated combination of word processor and printer, making use of microcomputer, software program and laser printer. The advantages for the small publisher are its high quality output, flexibility in terms of presentation, savings in time and money. This last factor is likely to continue as the costs of laser printers drop and there is further development in the software programs available.

Existing software packages allow the operator, who may also be author or editor, to generate text either directly by typing on to the screen, or by transferring from a word processor program. Different type faces, type sizes and graphics can be brought together on the screen, and the layout of the printed page can be tried out, moved around, and changed; and there will be no need for any manual intervention and paste-up. An increasingly large number of varied publishing products are now appearing as the result of DTP without any noticeable loss of quality, and this trend is expected to continue. Within a decade it is anticipated that most businesses will be their own publishers of office documents from brochures to expenses forms, and most associations, societies and small organizations will be publishers of their own newsletters, reports, handbooks.

It must be emphasized, however, that DTP does not come about as a simple operation where skills are not required because the computer takes care of all. It is true that the particular skills of the old traditional printing industry are no longer required. Instead responsibility for the printing processes now rests with those who are already undertaking the intellectual processes of writing and editing: indeed to operate DTP successfully requires all the skills, imagination, energy and business acumen of writer, editor, compositor and print-room manager rolled into one.

Articles about DTP are appearing in professional journals and a certain amount of current information is available and is being updated continuously: recent publications include:

Miles	*Design for desktop publishing*, 1987	222
Hartnell	*Desktop publishing: the book*, 1987	223

Printing in quantities For 'in-house' and DTP operations existing facilities within the organization may be sufficient to undertake the reproduction of copies; that is, by making use of the larger types of copying machines which can copy on both sides of a sheet, can sort and collate sheets. In many organizations larger copying machines may have periods of little use and could economically and efficiently take over the production of brochures and reports. The qualifications should be, in making use of such machines, not too many pages and not too many copies.

When the number of copies or size of the publication is likely to be extensive it is better to make use of the services of commercial printers with high speed sophisticated off-set machines; at the same time making use of the advice on technical matters such as weight of paper, thickness of cover, style of spine binding, which printers are competent and pleased to give.

3.5 Binding the document

The binding processes comprise the various methods by which the leaves, sections, printed sheets, are held together and fixed so that they will be usable and resistant to wear over a prolonged period. Binding can take place directly after printing in the same establishment or separately at a bindery. At the same time as part of a series of mechanized processes books may be given dustjackets and books and journals may be wrapped ready for mailing. The binding processes are folding, gathering, sewing and/or glueing, trimming and attaching a cover.

Binding was once a craft and an artistic skill, but little of this hand craftmanship now remains except in the repair and binding of antiquarian books, in the binding of special edition books, and as a hobby. Manuals about hand-binding and practical guides include:

Burdett	*The craft of bookbinding*, 1983	224
Johnson	*Manual of bookbinding*, 1978	225
Smith	*New directions in book binding*, 1974	226

The most widely used method of binding today for journals and paperbacks is the so called 'perfect binding', where the sheets are glued directly to the spine without any stitching.

To match the interest in 'in-house' printing operations, 'in-house' methods of binding have been developed; some of these make use of glue and heat (thermal binding), others use spiral ring binding. The equipment is generally desk top size, hand-operated, and the end product, though it may not have a long life, will make an attractive presentation of a report.

Recently conservation policies directed at helping to preserve older library collections have become more intensive, and attention has turned, as one aspect of conservation, to preserving older bindings: an example of one of the manuals published by a library association for this purpose is the American Library Association's:

| Middleton | *The restoration of leather bindings*, 2nd rev. ed., 1984 | 227 |

4 PRODUCING DOCUMENTS IN MICROFORM

While documents produced in print on paper remain those most widely in use there will be occasions when the decision is taken by editor or publisher to produce text in microform, in the belief that the advantages outweigh the obvious disadvantages. The particular appeal of microform is for publications which are distributed on a regular basis and which in print and on paper would be bulky to package and expensive to mail: that is, serials, both primary journals and the regularly distributed services of the abstracting and indexing organizations; handbooks and reference guides that are regularly updated by issue or by page. In these cases the advantages for the publisher and distributor are apparent, particularly that of economy, and there are also advantages for reader and user in that an updated microfiche is easier to consult than an out of date printed volume with supplements attached. In some instances both printed volumes and issues in microfiche are available to subscribers, but there has been a recent tendency to make the subscription rates for the 'hard copy' issues very much higher than for the microfiche versions, thus handicapping libraries in countries where the equipment for using microforms is not readily available.

In libraries, archives and information services the advantages of microform editions are also apparent:

- microfilming of archival material enables it to be used without wear and tear;
- microfilm and microfiche cannot be torn, creased, and will not fade;
- vast areas of storage space are released for other uses;
- microform material is easily stored where it is wanted;
- microforms can be duplicated easily and cheaply.

The disadvantages are generally with the reader: equipment is required. In some libraries the number of microform readers may be limited and may not always work, and there can be an additional strain in using the reader.

The actual filming of material to be reproduced in microform can be carried out within an organization, but is more generally undertaken by experts in the form of a microfilming bureau or service. Such an organization will undertake all the operations on site or on its own premises and will also guarantee the quality of the filming processes, checking for legibility, accuracy and density. Such bureaux will also attend scrupulously to matters of security and legality, and will issue certificates stating that each document received has been recorded in its original state.

A number of international standards dealing with microforms, prepared by ISO/TC 171, Micrographics, have been agreed; most of them concerned with the dimensions and quality determination in filming are very technical, addressed at the manufacturers. Equivalent British Standards have been prepared also. There is an ISO standard which provides guidance on the specialist vocabulary of micrographics, giving terms in English and French.

The ISO standards have been brought together in:

> ISO *Standards Handbook 1: Information transfer*, 2nd ed., 1982 23

Background information and surveys of equipment and applications can be found in:

> Baker *Micrographics year book*, 1987 228

4.1 Microfilming

The actual technique of microfilming begins with the recording of the original on film, which is usually 16mm or 35mm. The 35mm film is preferred for large-scale or difficult size original documents, such as engineering and architectural drawings and newspapers. The 16mm roll film is generally used for the microfilming of books, journals, dissertations, which are the kinds of documents most in demand in libraries worldwide.

The quality of the microfilm depends to a large extent on the quality of the original document, and there are always likely to be problems in legibility and exactness when the original is old, tattered or faded. Success in reproducing such fragile material depends very largely upon the skill of the microfilm unit and the quality of its cameras.

It is also very important that there is clear identification in the microfilm of the original document, and various efforts are underway to standardize the way in which microfilms are titled.

Microfiche Microfiche is a type of microfilm which has been increasingly used in recent years, but which originated as long ago as microfilm. One reason for its increased use has been the application of microfiche in the United States by the National Technical Information Service for the storage and distribution of its scientific and technical reports. Microfiche is also particularly useful for subscription services where there is a continuing process of updating: two examples are the issues of the *International Serials Data System Register* and the issues of *British Books in Print*. Micropublication is one of the major applications of microfiche today, and covers a wide range of large-scale publications, such as library catalogues, out of print long run serials, specialist collections of documents or pamphlets.

Computer output microfilm (COM) The application of film instead of paper printout from the computer is a special field of microfilming which has developed extremely rapidly. Roll film as well as microfiche can be used as a form of computer output microfilm (COM), although the trend is towards using microfiche. COM catalogues have become a familiar feature in libraries in many countries.

4.2 Using microforms

As already noted, microforms can only be used with specifically designed equipment, a microfilm or microfiche reader.

Over the years much research and development have gone into trying to design machines that are best suited to users' needs so as to overcome what is recognized as an initial reluctance to sitting in front of a machine concentrating on a screen. A wide range of microfilm and microfiche readers is now manufactured and new models are continually appearing on the market, offering further advantages of ease of use, better screen luminance, smaller size, cheaper. There are now available reader/printers which not only show the microfiche on the screen but which at a touch of a button can produce an immediate printout. Surveys of new equipment and new models are provided in journals and in year books: for example:

> *International journal of micrographics and video*   205
> *technology*
> Baker   *Micrographics year book*, 1987   228

As well as the special equipment required to use microforms, they have to be stored where possible in conditions which will not affect the quality of film, which may mean an air-conditioned room, and which is secure and fireproof; for example, in sealed containers, vacuum steel boxes, or in cardboard boxes in a safe. A range of storage containers is on the market. When in use, microfilm and microfiche are usually mounted into aperture cards or on to laminated jackets, which then require labelling and indexing. A microfilm bureau, as part of its service, will prepare film or fiche ready for use.

5 PRODUCING A DOCUMENT WITH ACCOMPANYING MATERIALS

For some purposes the author in consultation with editor and publisher may decide that a document will best suit its intended audience if it comprises several parts, one of text and one or more which may not be in a textual form: for example, a textbook designed for classroom use may be made up of students' test cards and teacher's handbook; a published article may also be required for presentation at a seminar and may best be used with some audio-visual aids. There are publications which are not strictly documents, although often produced by book publishers and found in bookshops, which are made up of a box with a game and explanatory brochure; or found in museum shops, a learning kit made up of maps and pieces of rock and an illustrated booklet. Specialist publications of this kind are likely to be prepared in close consultation of editor and publisher and with full awareness of the kind of specialist manufacturer and packaging required.

Consideration is given in this chapter to the more simple type of publication of a document with some accompanying materials which come into existence because author and editor believe that the document will be enhanced by the addition of audio-visual aids. It should be appreciated immediately that the addition of such aids brings a new dimension into the use of the document; that is, equipment will be required which affects where and how the document can be used and presented, the audience it can reach, and its price. The range of audio-visual aids is limited, but the range of different types of equipment to make use of audio-visual aids is vast. A summary is given here of some different kinds of audio-visual materials with an indication of the type of equipment required, from the simple and cheap to the more specialist:

- transparencies on acetate or plastic sheets   to be used with: overhead projector / projection screen
- 35mm photographic slides   to be used with: slide projector / projection screen / hand viewer

- audio recording on   to be used with: open reel tape
  open reel tapes or   recorder
  cassette tapes   tape cassette
                                                                              recorder
                                                                              microphone
- video recording   to be used with: television set
                                                                              video recorder

A useful guide to the use of audio-visual aids in the specialist subject field of library and information science training has been published by Unesco:

> Thompson   *Guide to the production and*   103
>   *use of audiovisual aids*, 1983

which also gives practical advice on making slides, transparencies and video recordings, and how best to present these as part of a teaching programme.

POSTSCRIPT

One volume with contents which cover many of the topics noted in these three chapters – and much more – is:

> Dear   *Oxford English: a guide to the*   229
>   *language*, 1986

with sections on foreign alphabets, punctuation, abbreviations and acronyms, grammar, speechmaking and toasts, slang, scientific writing, weights and measures, proof correction marks, computer terms, chemical elements; and in addition sections on classical literature, Dr Johnson, a short dictionary of literary figures. It is comprehensive and entertaining, a pleasant mixture of guide, encyclopaedia and bedside companion.

Bibliography

References to publications are presented in the numerical order of their first appearance in the text and with sufficient information to identify the publications in library catalogues or booksellers' lists.

The names of authors and editors are noted with initials; places as well as names of publishers are provided and dates of publication. Pagination is also given wherever possible and serves as a useful guide not just to the sizes of the publications but also to possible costs. Some of the titles listed have been prepared and published by non-commercial publishers and may not be available through the usual book trade channels but by direct application to the organization. The full addresses of the International Organization for Standardization, the British Standards Institution, and Unesco are given on p. 131.

The references are set out making use of the 'prescribed punctuation' and spacing currently used in bibliographic records prepared by national and international library and information services.

1 International Organization for Standardization (ISO)
International standard vocabularies. – 4th ed. – Geneva : ISO, 1986. – 40p. – (ISO bibliographies ; 8)

2 ISO
ISO 6156–1987 Magnetic tape exchange for-

mat for terminological/lexicographical records (MATER). – Geneva : ISO, 1987. – 25p.

3 Krommer-Benz, Magdalena
International bibliography of computer-assisted terminology. – Paris : Unesco : Infoterm, 1984. – 36p. – (PGI–84/WS/12)

4 Felbert, Helmut
Terminology manual. – Paris : Unesco : Infoterm, 1984. – 426p. – (PGI–84/WS/21)

5 ISO
ISO 704–1987   Principles and methods of terminology. – Geneva : ISO, 1987. – 16p.

6 ISO
ISO/DP860–1987   International unification of concepts and terms   [DP = Draft Proposal]

7 ISO
ISO/DP919–1987   Guide for the preparation of classified vocabularies

8 ISO
ISO/DP1987–1987   Vocabulary of terminology

9 ISO
ISO/DP1149–1987   Layout of multilingual classified vocabularies

10 ISO
ISO/DP1951–1987   Lexicographical symbols for use in classified defining vocabularies

11 ISO
ISO/DP4466–1987   Layout of monolingual classified vocabularies

12 ISO
ISO 3166–1981   Codes for the representation of names of countries. – 2nd ed. – Geneva : ISO, 1981. – 49p. – Bilingual edition in English and French.

Bibliography

13 British Standards Institution (BSI)
BS 5374–1981 Specification for codes for the representation of names of countries. – Milton Keynes : BSI, 1981. – 56p.

14 ISO
ISO/DIS639–1987 Code for the representation of names of languages : bilingual edition [DIS = Draft International Standard]

15 ISO
ISO 5127–1981–83 Documentation and information : vocabulary. – Geneva : ISO, 1981–83. – 5 parts.
- Part 1: Basic concepts, 1983
- Part 2: Traditional documents, 1983
- Part 3a: Acquisition, identification and analysis of documents and data, 1981
- Part 6: Documentary languages, 1983
- Part 11: Audio-visual documents, 1983

16 BSI
BS 5408–1976 Glossary of documentation terms. – Milton Keynes : BSI, 1976. – 88p. – Covers Parts 1, 2, 3a, 6, 11 of ISO 5127.

17 ISO
ISO/DIS5127–1987
- Part 3: Iconic documents
- Part 4: Archival documents
- Part 7: Retrieval and dissemination of information
- Part 8: Reprography of documents

18 ISO
ISO Standards Handbook 10 : Data processing – vocabulary. – Geneva : ISO, 1982. – 360p. –

Text in English and French includes all parts of ISO 2382.
19 Bennett, Paul A. *and others*
Multilingual aspects of information technology. – Aldershot, Hants : Gower Publishing, 1986. – 160p.
20 International Federation of Automatic Control
Multilingual glossary of automatic control technology : English, French, German, Russian, Italian, Spanish, Japanese. – Oxford : Pergamon Press for the International Federation of Automatic Control, 1981. – Paged in sections.
21 The Multilingual business handbook : a guide to international correspondence : Deutsch : English (including American English) : Español : Français : Italiano. – London : Pan Books, 1983. – 347p.
22 Room, A.
Dictionary of translated names and titles. – London : Routledge & Kegan Paul, 1986. – 460p. – 6 languages, English, French, German, Italian, Spanish, Russian.
23 ISO
ISO Standards Handbook 1 : Information transfer. – 2nd ed. – Geneva : ISO, 1982. – 522p.
24 Chambers 20th century dictionary / edited by E. M. Kirkpatrick. – New ed. – Edinburgh : Chambers, 1987. – 1583p.
25 The Concise Oxford dictionary of current English. – 7th ed. / edited by J. B. Sykes, 1982. – Oxford : Clarendon Press, 1987. – 1260p.
26 The New Collins concise dictionary of the English language. – London : Collins, 1987. – 1388p.
27 Webster's Ninth New Collegiate dictionary. – Spring-

Bibliography

field, Mass : Merriam-Webster, 1987. – 1563p.
28 The Oxford reference dictionary / edited by J. M. Hawkins ; illustrations edited by S. LeRoux. – Oxford : Clarendon Press, 1986. – 972p.
29 Roget's Thesaurus. – New edition / prepared by B. Kirkpatrick. – London : Longman, 1987. – 1247p.
30 The Penguin modern guide to synonyms and related words / edited by S. I. Hayakawa ; revised by P. J. Fletcher. – London : Penguin, 1987. – 707p.
31 The Oxford dictionary for writers and editors / compiled by The Oxford English Dictionary Department. – Oxford : Clarendon Press, 1986. – 448p.
32 Fowler, H. W.
A dictionary of modern English usage. – 2nd ed. rev. / by E. Gowers. – London : Oxford University Press, 1987. – 725p.
33 Partridge, Eric
Usage and abusage : a guide to good English. – New edition. – London : Book Club Associates, 1982. – 392p. – First edition, 1942.
34 Gowers, Ernest
The complete plain words / revised by S. Greenbaum and J. Whitcut. – London : HMSO, 1986. – 288p. – First edition, 1954.
35 Phythian, B.A.
A concise dictionary of correct English. – London : Hodder & Stoughton, 1987. – 166p. – Based on Fowler, Gowers and others.
36 Strunk, W.
The elements of style. – New edition of 3rd ed. / by E. B. White. – London : Collier Macmillan, 1982. – 112p.

37 Todd, L. *and* Hancock, I.
International English usage. – London : Croom Helm, 1986. – 520p.
38 Cowie, A. P. *and* Mackin, R.
Oxford dictionary of current idiomatic English. – London : Oxford University Press, 1985. – 2v. – Contents: V.1: Verbs with prepositions and participles; V.2: Phrase, clause and sentence idioms.
39 The Oxford guide to the English language. – London : Oxford University Press, 1985. – 577p. – Contents: Oxford guide to English usage / by E. S. C. Weiner; Dictionary.
40 Quirk, R. *and others*
A grammar of contemporary English. – London : Longman, 1987. – 1120p.
41 Leech, G. *and* Svartvik, J.
A communicative grammar of English. – London : Longman, 1987. – 484p.
42 Quirk, R. *and* Greenbaum, S.
A university grammar of English. – London : Longman, 1987. – 484p.
43 Carey, G. V.
Mind the stop : a brief guide to punctuation, with a note on proof-correction. – Harmondsworth : Penguin Books, 1986.
44 Partridge, E.
You have a point there : a guide to punctuation and its allies. – London : Routledge & Kegan Paul, 1983. – 230p.
45 Pugh, E.
Pugh's Dictionary of acronyms and abbreviations. – 5th ed. – London : Library Association; Chicago : American Library Association, 1987.
46 Elsevier's foreign-language teacher's dictionary of

Bibliography

47 ISO
acronyms and abbreviations / edited by Jung. – Amsterdam : Elsevier, 1985. – 138p.

ISO 4–1984 Rules for the abbreviation of title words and titles of publications. – 3rd ed. – Geneva : ISO, 1984.

48 British Standards Institution (BSI)
BS 4148–1985 Specifications for the abbreviation of title words and titles of publication. – Milton Keynes : BSI, 1985.

49 International Serials Data System (ISDS)
List of serial title word abbreviations. – Paris : ISDS International Centre, 1985.

50 ISO
ISO Standards Handbook 2 : Units of measurement [SI units and recommendations for their use]. – 2nd ed. – Geneva : ISO, 1982. – 264p.

51 BSI
BS 5775–1979–82 [Equivalent of 13 parts of ISO 31]

52 ISO
ISO Standards Handbook 3 : Statistical methods. – 2nd ed. – Geneva : ISO, 1981. – 456p.

53 ISO
ISO 4217–1987 Codes for the representation of currencies and funds. – Geneva : ISO, 1987. – 45p. – Bilingual edition, English and French.

54 ISO
ISO 5966–1982 Presentation of scientific and technical reports. – Geneva : ISO, 1982. – 22p.

55 ISO
ISO 7144–1986 Presentation of theses and similar documents. – Geneva : ISO, 1986. – 10p.

56 BSI
BS 4821–1972 (1986) Recommendation for

57 ISO
the presentation of theses. – Milton Keynes : BSI, 1972. – 12p.

ISO 215–1986 Presentation of contributions to periodicals and other serials. – Geneva : ISO, 1986. – 5p.

58 BSI
BS 2509–1970 (1983) Specification for the presentation of serial publications including periodicals. – Milton Keynes : BSI, 1970. – Incorporating ISO 8, Presentation of periodicals.

59 Booth, V.
Writing a scientific paper. – 4th ed. rev. – Colchester, Essex : Biochemical Society Book Depot, 1978.

60 Mathes, J. C. *and* Stevenson, D. W.
Designing technical reports : writing for audiences in organizations. – Indianapolis : Bobbs-Merrill, 1976. – 396p.

61 Mitchell, J.
How to write reports. – London : Fontana, 1974. – 160p.

62 Mort, S.
How to write a successful report. – New ed. – London : Business Books, 1984. – 280p.

63 Sussams, J. E.
How to write effective reports. – Aldershot, Hants : Gower Publishing, 1983. – 120p. – (Management skills library).

64 Turabian, K. L.
A manual for writers of research papers, theses and dissertations. – London : Heinemann, 1982. – 240p. – First published 1967.

65 The ALA glossary of library and information science / Heartsill Young, editor [and others]. – Chicago :

American Library Association, 1983. – 245p.
66 Harrod's Librarians' glossary and reference book of terms used in librarianship, documentation and the book crafts. – 6th ed. – Aldershot, Hants : Gower Publishing, 1987. – 868p.
67 Isaacs, A. *ed.*
The Penguin dictionary of science. – 6th rev. ed. – Harmondsworth : Penguin Books, 1986. – 544p.
68 Stiegler, S. E. *ed.*
Dictionary of economics and business. – 2nd ed. – Aldershot, Hants : Gower Publishing, 1985. – 470p.
69 Chambers science and technology dictionary. – New ed. – Edinburgh : W. & R. Chambers, 1984. – 1328p.
70 Horner, C. F. *and* Liebster, L. M.
Newnes pocket dictionary of business terms. – Feltham, Middx : Newnes Books, 1984. – 317p.
71 O'Connor, M. *and* Woodford, F. P.
Writing scientific books in English. – New ed. – London : Pitman Medical Books, 1978. – 108p.
72 Booth, V.
Communicating in science : writing and speaking. – London : Cambridge University Press, 1985. – 68p.
73 Calnan, J. *and* Barabas, A.
Writing medical papers : a practical guide. – London : Heinemann Medical Books, 1973. – 112p.
74 King, L. S.
Why not say it clearly? A guide to scientific writing. – New York : Little Brown, 1978. – 186p.

75 Kirkman, J.
Good style for scientific and engineering writing. – London : Pitman, 1980. – 131p.

76 Thorne, C.
Thorne's Better medical writing. – 2nd ed. / revised by S. Lock. – London : Pitman Medical Books, 1977. – 118p.

77 Trelease, S. F.
How to write scientific and technical papers. – Cambridge, Mass : MIT Press, 1969. – 200p. – First published 1958.

78 American Institute of Physics (AIP)
Style manual. – 3rd ed. – New York : AIP, 1978.

79 American Psychological Association (APA)
Publication manual. – 2nd ed. – Washington DC : APA, 1974.

80 Council of Biology Editors (CBE)
CBE style manual. – 4th ed. – Arlington, Va : American Institute of Biological Sciences, 1978. – 265p.

81 Royal Society
General notes on the preparation of scientific papers. – 3rd ed. – London : RS, 1974. – 31p.

82 Modern Humanities Research Association (MHRA)
MHRA style book : notes for authors, editors and writers of dissertations. – 3rd ed. – London : MHRA, 1986. – 73p.

83 Hartley, J.
Designing instructional text. – 2nd ed. rev. – London : Kogan Page, 1985. – 125p.

84 Pickens, J. E.
The copy-to-press handbook : preparing words and art for print. – New York : Wiley, 1985. – 547p.

85 White, J. V.
Editing by design : a guide to effective word-and-picture communication for editors and designers. – 2nd ed. – New York : Bowker, 1982. – 248p.
86 Wood, P.
Scientific illustration : a guide to biological, zoological and medical rendering techniques, design, printing and display. – New ed. – New York : Van Nostrand Reinhold, 1982.
87 United Nations. Department of Conference Services
United Nations editorial manual : a compendium of rules and directives on United Nations editorial style, publication policies, procedures and practices. – New York : United Nations ; London : HMSO [distributor], 1983. – 524p.
88 ISO
ISO Standards Handbook 12 : Technical drawings. – Geneva : ISO, 1982. – 350p.
89 ISO
ISO 710–1974–84   Graphical symbols for use on detailed maps, plans and geological cross-sections. – Geneva : ISO, 1974–84. – 7 parts.
90 ISO
ISO Standards Handbook 9 : Data processing : software. – Geneva : ISO, 1982. – 439p.
91 Dunckel, J. *and* Parnham, E.
The business guide to effective speaking. – London : Kogan Page, 1985. – 122p.
92 Janner, G.
Janner's Complete speechmaker. – 2nd ed. – London : Business Books, 1986. – 301p.
93 Calnan, J. *and* Barabas, A.
Speaking at medical meetings : a practical guide. – 2nd rev. ed. – London : Heinemann Medical Books, 1981. – 200p.

94 Dixon, D. *and* Hills, P.
    Talking about your research. – Leicester : University of Leicester, 1981. – 36p.
95 Drain, R. *and* Oakley, N.
    Successful conference and convention planning. – Toronto : McGraw-Hill Ryerson, 1978. – 205p.
96 Jax, J. L.
    Blueprint for success : a manual for conventions, conferences, seminars and workshops. – Madison : Wisconsin Library Association, 1981.
97 Loughary, J. W. *and* Hopson, B.
    Producing workshops, seminars and short courses : a trainer's handbook. – Chicago : Association Press, 1979. – 202p.
98 Lowry-Corry, E.
    Let's have a conference! – London : Aslib, 1987.
99 Seekings, D.
    How to organize effective conferences and meetings. – 3rd ed. – London : Kogan Page, 1987. – 225p.
100 International Association of Professional Conference Organizers (IAPCO)
    Glossary of conference terminology : a manual for organizers for use mainly in the preparation of multilingual printed conference manual [i.e. materials]. – Brussels : IAPCO, 1980. – In 5 languages, English, German, French, Spanish, Italian.
101 Unesco
    Glossary of conference terms (English–French–Arabic). – 2nd rev. ed. – Paris : Unesco, 1980. – 287p.
102 Citrine's ABC of chairmanship / edited by M. Cannell

and N. Citrine. – 4th ed. – London : NCLC Publishing Society, 1982. – 122p.
103 Thompson, A. H.
Guide to the production and use of audio-visual aids in library and information science teaching. – Paris : Unesco, 1983. – 125p. – (PGI–83/WS/17).
104 Cullen, P. *and* Kirby, J.
Design and production of media presentations for libraries. – Aldershot, Hants : Gower Publishing, 1986. – 96p.
105 The book publishing annual : highlights, analyses, trends. – New York : Bowker, 1985.
106 Taubert, S. *and* Weidhass, P. *ed.*
The book trade of the world. – Munich : Saur, 1972–84. – 4v. –
Contents: Vol. 1: Europe and international section
Vol. 2: The Americas, Australia, New Zealand
Vol. 3: Asia
Vol. 4: Africa; with index
107 Willing's press guide : a guide to the press of the United Kingdom and the principal publications of Europe, the Americas, Australasia, the Far East and the Middle East. – East Grinstead, Sussex : Thomas Skinner Directories, 1987.
108 Legat, M.
An author's guide to publishing. – New ed. – London : Robert Hale, 1987. – 192p.
109 Wells, G.
The successful author's handbook. – London : Macmillan, 1981. – 166p.
110 Finch, P.
How to publish yourself. – London : W. H. Allen, 1987. – 143p.

111 Fluegelman, A. *and* Hewes, J. J.
Writing in the computer age : word processing skills and style for every writer. – London : Century publishing, 1983. – 256p.

112 Hammond, R.
The writer and the word processor : a guide for authors, journalists, poets and playwrights. – London : Hodder & Stoughton, 1984. – 224p.

113 Holloway, H. L.
Author-generated phototypesetting : author/publisher/printer links. – Oxford : Elsevier International Bulletins, 1985. – 80p.

114 O'Connor, M.
Model guidelines for the preparation of camera-ready typescripts by authors and typists : including bibliographical references in scientific publications. – London : Ciba Foundation, 1980. – 47p.

115 ICSU–CODATA Task Group
Study on the problems of accessibility and dissemination of data for science and technology. – Paris : Unesco, 1974. – 102p. – (SC/14/

116 BSI
BS 2846–1985 Guide to statistical interpretation of data. – Milton Keynes : BSI, 1985. – 7 parts.

117 ICSU–CODATA Task Group
Guide for the presentation in the primary literature of numerical data derived from experiments. – Paris : Unesco, 1974.

118 Rossmassler, S. A. *and* Watson, D. G. *ed.*
Data handling for science and technology : an overview and source book. – Amsterdam : North Holland, 1980. – 184p.

119 Chen, C. C. *and* Hernon, P. *ed.*
Numeric data bases. – Ablex Publishers, 1984. – 332p.
120 The Chicago manual of style : for authors, editors, and copywriters. – 13th ed. revised and expanded. – Chicago : University Press, 1982. – 738p.
121 Hart, H.
Hart's rules : for compositors and readers at the University Press, Oxford. – 39th ed. completely revised. – London : Oxford University Press, 1983. – 182p.
122 Bodian, N. G.
Copywriter's handbook : professional editing and publishing. – Philadelphia, PA : ISI Press, 1984.
123 Butcher, J.
Copy-editing : the Cambridge handbook. – 2nd rev. ed. – Cambridge : University Press, 1983. – 332p.
124 The Economist pocket style book. – London : The Economist Publications, 1986. – 96p.
125 American Library Association (ALA)
Guidelines for authors, editors and publishers of literature in the library and information field. – Chicago : ALA, 1983.
126 American Medical Association (AMA)
Style book and editorial manual. – 5th ed. – Chicago : AMA, 1971.
127 Editerra editors' handbook. – Franham, Surrey : Editerra, 1977.
128 Modern Language Association of America (MLAA)
Statement of editorial principles and procedures : a working manual for editing nineteenth century American texts. – Rev. ed. – New York : MLAA, 1972.

129 O'Connor, M.
Editing scientific books and journals : an ELSE–Ciba Foundation guide for editors. – London : Pitman Medical Books, 1978. – 218p.

130 O'Connor, M.
How to copyedit scientific books and journals. – Philadelphia, PA : ISI Press, 1986. – 150p.

131 Arnold, E.C.
Editing the organizational publication. – Ragan Communication, 1982. – 284p.

132 Bentley, G.
Editing the company publication. – New ed. – London : Greenwood Pubs., 1975. – 242p. – First published 1953.

133 Beach, M.
Editing your newsletter : a guide to writing, design and production. – 2nd rev. ed. – New York : Van Nostrand Reinhold, 1983. – 128p.

134 Ferguson, R.
Editing the small magazine. – 2nd ed. – New York : Columbia University Press, 1976. – 221p.

135 Wales, L. H.
A practical guide to newsletter editing and design : instructions for printing by mimeograph or offset for the inexperienced editor. – 2nd ed. – Ames : Iowa State University Press, 1976. – 50p.

136 DeBakey, L.
The scientific journal : editorial policies and practices : guidelines for editors, reviewers and authors. – St Louis, Mo : Mosby, 1976. – 129p.

137 Swanson, E.
Mathematics into type. – Rev. ed. – Provi-

dence, RI : American Mathematical Society, 1982. – 98p.
138 Unesco
Style manual for the presentation of English-language manuscripts intended for publication by Unesco. – Paris : Unesco, 1981. – 67p.
139 Grünewald, H.
Guidelines for editors of scientific and technical journals. – Paris : Unesco, 1979. – 36p. – (PGI–79/WS/8).
140 Martinsson, A.
Guide for the preparation of scientific papers for publication. – 2nd ed. – Paris : Unesco, 1983. – 13p. – (PGI–83/WS/10).
141 ISO
ISO 8–1977   Presentation of periodicals. – Geneva : ISO, 1977. – 4p.
142 Burbidge, P. G.
Prelims and end-pages. – 2nd ed. – London : Cambridge University Press, 1969. – 31p. – (Cambridge authors' and printers' guides : 7).
143 ISO
ISO 6357–1985   Spine titles on books and other publications. – Geneva : ISO, 1985.
144 BSI
BS 6738–1986   Recommendations for presentation of spine titles. – Milton Keynes : BSI, 1986.
145 ISO
ISO/DP1086–1987   Title-leaves of books
146 ISO
ISO 18–1981   Contents list of periodicals. – Geneva : ISO, 1981.
147 ISO
ISO 214–1976   Abstracts for publication and documentation. – Geneva : ISO, 1976.

148 ISO
ISO 5122–1979   Abstract sheets in serial publications. – Geneva : ISO, 1979.
149 Borko, H. *and* Bernier, C. L.
Abstracting concepts and methods. – New York : Academic Press, 1975. – 250p.
150 Cremmins, E. T.
The art of abstracting. – Philadelphia, PA : ISI Press, 1982. – 150p.
151 Maizell, R. *and others*
Abstracting scientific and technical literature : an introductory guide and text for scientists, abstractors, and management. – New York : Wiley, 1979. – 316p.
152 Rowley, J.
Abstracting and indexing. – London : Bingley, 1982. – 155p.
153 American Chemical Society (ACS)
Directions for abstractors and section editors of Chemical Abstracts Service. – Columbus, Ohio : ACS, 1971. – 62p.
154 Burbidge, P. G.
Notes and references. – Cambridge : University Press, 1952. – (Cambridge authors' and printers' guides).
155 ISO
ISO 690–1987   Bibliographic references : content, form and structure. – Geneva : ISO, 1987.
156 ISO
ISO 9115–1987   Bibliographic identification (biblid) of contributions in serials and books. – Geneva : ISO, 1987.
157 ISO
ISO 999–1975   Index of a publication. – Geneva : ISO, 1975.

158 BSI
> BS 3700-1976 (1983) Recommendations : the preparation of indexes to books, periodicals and other publications. – Milton Keynes : BSI, 1976. – 16p.

159 Anderson, M. D.
> Book indexing. – Cambridge : University Press, 1987. – 37p. – (Cambridge authors' and printers' guides).

160 Knight, G. N.
> Indexing, the art of : a guide to the indexing of books and periodicals. – London : Allen & Unwin, 1983. – 218p.

161 Butcher, J.
> Typescript, proofs and indexes : a guide for authors. – Cambridge : University Press, 1980. – 32p. – (Cambridge authors' and printers' guides).

162 Borko, H. *and* Bernier, C. L.
> Indexing concepts and methods. – New York : Academic Press, 1979. – 261p.

163 ISO
> ISO 2108-1978 International Standard Book Numbering. – Geneva : ISO, 1978.

164 ISO
> ISO 3297-1984 International Standard Serial Numbering. – 3rd ed. – Geneva : ISO, 1984.

165 Anderson, D.
> Guidelines for cataloguing-in-publication. – Paris : Unesco, 1986. – 83p. – (PGI-86/WS/1).

166 Lunn, J.
> Guidelines for legal deposit legislation. – Paris : Unesco, 1981. – 33p. – (PGI-81/WS/23).

167 Unesco
The ABC of copyright. – Paris : Unesco, 1981. – 73p.
168 Cavendish, J. M.
A handbook of copyright in British publishing practice. – 2nd ed. rev. – London : Cassell, 1984. – 210p.
169 Davies, G.
Challenge to copyright and related rights in the European Community. – Oxford : ESC Publishing, 1983. – 300p.
170 DeFreitas, D.
The copyright system : practice and problems in developing countries. – London : Commonwealth Secretariat, 1983.
171 Stewart, S. M.
International copyright and neighbouring rights. – London : Butterworths, 1983. – 740p.
172 Weil, B. M.
Modern copyright fundamentals. – New York : Van Nostrand Reinhold, 1985. – 480p.
173 Munce, H.
Graphics handbook : a beginner's guide to design, copy fitting, and printing procedures. – North Light Pubs, 1982. – 160p.
174 Lewis, J.
Twentieth century book : its illustration and design. – 2nd ed. rev. – Herbert Press, 1984. – 272p.
175 Jacob, H.
A pocket dictionary of publishing terms including explanations and definitions of words and phrases commonly used in the production and distribution of books. – London : Macdonald, 1976. – 192p.

176 Orne, J.
    The language of the foreign book trade : abbreviations, terms, phrases. – 3rd. ed. – Chicago : American Library Association, 1976. – 454p. – Includes terms in 14 languages.

177 Isaacs, A. *ed.*
    The multilingual dictionary of printing and publishing. – New York : Facts on file, 1981. – 289p.

178 Evans, H. *ed.*
    Editing and design : a five-volume manual of English typography and layout. – 2nd ed. – London : Heinemann for the National Council for the Training of Journalists, 1972–78 (reprint 1982). –
    Contents: Bk. 1: Newsman's English
             Bk. 2: Handling newspaper text
             Bk. 3: News headlines
             Bk. 4: Picture editing
             Bk. 5: Newspaper design

179 Williamson, H.
    Methods of book design : the practice of an industrial craft. – 3rd. ed. – New York : Yale University Press, 1983. – 392p. – First published 1956.

180 Seybold, J. W.
    Fundamentals of modern photocomposition. – Media, PA : Seybold Publications, 1979.

181 Seybold, J. W.
    World of digital typesetting. – Media, PA : Seybold Publications, 1984.

182 Bodian, N. G.
    Book marketing handbook : tips and techniques for the sale and promotion of scientific, technical, professional and scholarly books

and journals. – New York : Bowker, 1980–83. – 2v.
183 Day, R. A.
How to write and publish a scientific paper. – 2nd ed. – Philadelphia, PA : ISI Press, 1984. – 181p.
184 Powell, W. W.
Getting into print : the decision making process in scholarly publishing. – Chicago : University of Chicago Press, 1985. – 260p.
185 Smith, K.
Marketing for small publishers. – London : InterChange Books, 1980. – 131p.
186 BSI
BS 5261–1975–6   Guide to copy preparation and proof correction. – Milton Keynes : BSI, 1975–76. – 2 pts. –
Contents: Pt. 1: Recommendations for preparation of typescript copy for printing
Pt. 2: Specifications for typographic requirements, marks for copy preparation and proof correction, proofing procedure.
187 Hills, P. *ed.*
The future of the printed word : the impact and the implications of the new communications technology. – Milton Keynes : Open University, 1981.
188 Gibson, M. L.
Editing in the electronic era. – 2nd ed. – Ames : Iowa State University Press, 1984.
189 Gurnsey, J.
The information professions in the electronic age. – London : Bingley, 1985. – 206p.

190 Derrick, J. *and* Oppenheim, P.
The word processing handbook. – London : Kogan Page, 1984. – 160p.
191 Wells, G.
Low-cost word processing. – London : Allison & Busby, 1986. – 138p.
192 Townsend, K. *and* Taphouse, K.
Word processing for solicitors. – Aldershot, Hants : Gower Publishing, 1983.
193 The international word processing report : news and technical guidance for the professional community involved with automated text production and modern systems for office efficiency. – New York : Geyer-McAllister Inter Inc., 1979. – Monthly.
194 Jonassen, D. H. *ed.*
The technology of text : principles for structuring, designing and displaying text. – Englewood Cliffs, NJ : Educational Technology Publications, 1982. – 478p.
195 Vollnhals, O. *comp.*
Elsevier's dictionary of word processing in three languages : English, French, German. – Amsterdam : Elsevier, 1986. – 303p.
196 Illingworth, V. *ed.*
Minidictionary of computing. – Oxford : University Press, 1986. – 294p.
197 Longley, D. *and* Shain, M.
Macmillan dictionary of information technology. – 2nd ed. – London : Macmillan, 1986. – 382p.
198 Meadows, A. J. *and others*
Dictionary of computing and information technology : guide for industry, business, education and the home. – 3rd ed. – London : Kogan Page, 1987. – 288p.

199 Sippl, C. J.
   Macmillan dictionary of microcomputing. – 3rd. ed. – London : Macmillan, 1985. – 473p.
200 Stokes, A. V.
   Concise encyclopaedia, of information technology. – 3rd ed. – Aldershot, Hants : Gower Publishing, 1986. – 279p.
201 The computer users' year book, 1988. – London : VNU Business Publications, 1987. – 4v.
202 Deighton, S. *and others*
   Computers and information processing world index. – Aldershot, Hants : Gower Publishing, 1984. – 616p.
203 Longley, D. *and* Shain, M.
   The microcomputer users' handbook 1985 : the complete and up to date guide to buying a business computer. – London : Macmillan Press, 1985. – 405p.
204 Information media and technology : the journal of Cimtech, the National Centre for Information Media and Technology. – Hatfield, Herts. : Cimtech, 1986– . – Formerly 'Reprographic quarterly'. – Issue seen V.19, no. 2. – Quarterly. ISSN 0266–6960.
205 International journal of micrographics and video technology. – Oxford : Pergamon Press, 1985– . – Formerly 'Microdoc' and 'Micropublishing of current periodicals'. – Issues seen V.4, no. 3/4. – Quarterly. – ISSN 0743–9636.
206 Microcomputers for information management : an international journal for library and information services. – Norwood, NJ : Ablex Publishing Corporation, 1985– . – Issue seen V.2, no. 4. – Quarterly. – ISSN 0742–2342.
207 Information processing and management : an international journal (incorporating 'Information

technology'). – Oxford : Pergamon Press, 1986– . – Issue seen V.22, no. 3. – Bi-monthly. – ISSN 0306–4573.

208 Condon, M. A.
Text creation in the electronic office. – Manchester : National Computer Centre Publications, 1983.

209 Greenberger, M. *ed.*
Electronic publishing plus : media for a technological future. – London : Knowledge Industry Publications, 1985. – 384p.

210 Nania, G. *comp.*
Complete multilingual dictionary of computer terminology (English, French, Italian, Spanish, Portuguese). – Lincolnwood (Chicago) : Passport Books, 1984. – 916p.

211 European Computer Manufacturers' Association (ECMA)
The meaning of conformance to standards. – Geneva : ECMA, 1983. – (ECMA/TR18 (1983)).

212 European Computer Manufacturers' Association (ECMA)
Safety requirements for data processing equipment. – 2nd ed. – Geneva : ECMA, 1981. – Prepared in association with International Electrotechnical Commission. – (ECMA–57).

213 European Computer Manufacturers' Association (ECMA)
Ergonomics – recommendations for VDU work places. – Geneva : ECMA, 1984. – (ECMA/TR22 (1984)).

214 Alder, D.
The bookman's book. – London : Inveresk Paper Group, 1969.

215 ISO
ISO 216-1975 Writing paper and certain classes of printed matter – Trimmed sizes – A and B series. – Geneva : ISO, 1975. [Also included in ISO Standards Handbook 1 (23)].

216 BSI
BS 4000-1983 Specification for size of paper and board. – Milton Keynes : BSI, 1983.

217 Morison, S.
First principles of typography. – 2nd ed. – London : Cambridge University Press, 1967. – (Cambridge authors' and printers' guides : 1).

218 Jennett, S.
The making of books. – 5th ed. – London : Faber, 1973.

219 British Printing Industries Federation (BPIF)
Printers' yearbook 1987-88 : the comprehensive guide to the printing industry. – London : BPIF, 1987. – 328p.

220 Smith, J. W. T. *and* Merali, Z.
Optical character recognition : the technology and its application in information units and libraries. – London : British Library, 1985. – (LIR Report 33).

221 Condon, M. A.
Office printers : a practical evaluation guide. – Manchester : National Computer Centre Publications, 1982. – 116p.

222 Miles, J.
Design for desktop publishing : a guide to layout and typography on the personal computer. – London : Gordon Fraser, 1987. – 103p.

223 Hartnell, T.
Desktop publishing : the book. – London : Interface Publications, 1987. – 160p.

224 Burdett, E.
The craft of bookbinding : a practical handbook. – Newton Abbot, Devon : David & Charles, 1983. – 400p.
225 Johnson, A. W.
Manual of bookbinding. – London : Thames & Hudson, 1978. – 224p.
226 Smith P.
New directions in book binding. – London : Studio Vista, 1974. – 208p.
227 Middleton, B. C.
The restoration of leather bindings. – 2nd ed. rev. – Chicago : Adamantine Press, 1984. – 220p.
228 Baker, G. G. *and others*
Micrographics year book 1987. – G. G. Baker & Associates, 1987. – 240p.
229 Dear, I. C. B. *comp.*
Oxford English : a guide to the language. – London : Guild Publishing, 1986. – 704p.

Useful addresses

For standards and standard practices generally:

International organizations:

    International Organization for Standardization (ISO)
        Central Secretariat
        CH–1211 Geneva 20
        Switzerland

    Unesco
        7 Place de Fontenoy
        75700 Paris
        France

In the United Kingdom:

    British Standards Institution (BSI)
        Linford Wood
        Milton Keynes MK14 6LA
        United Kingdom

In the United States of America:

    America National Standards Institute (ANSI)
        1430 Broadway
        New York NY 10018
        United States of America

National Bureau of Standards
Gaithersburg
Maryland MD 20899
United States of America

For standards and standard practices in documentation:

International organizations:

ISO Technical Committee 46, Documentation (ISO/TC46)
Secretariat
Deutsches Institut für Normung
Postfach 1107
D-1000 Berlin 30
Federal Republic of Germany

International Information Centre on Standards in Information and Documentation (ISODOC)
As above: the Secretariat of ISO/TC46

Unesco
General Information Programme (PGI)
7 Place de Fontenoy
75700 Paris
France

In the United States:

National Information Standards Organization Committee Z39, Library and Information Sciences and Related Publishing Practices (NISO-Z39)
National Bureau of Standards Administration 101
Gaithersburg
Maryland MD 20899
United States of America

For standards and standard practices in terminology:

ISO Technical Committee 37, Terminology
(ISO/TC37)
    Secretariat
    Osterreichisches Normunginstitut
    Postfach 130
    A–1021 Vienna
    Austria

International Information Centre for Terminology
(INFOTERM)
    As above: the Secretariat of ISO/TC37

For computing and computer standards:

International Electrotechnical Commission (IEC)
    1 rue Varembé
    CH–1211 Geneva
    Switzerland

Consultative Committee of the International Telecommunications Union (CCITT)
    Place des Nations
    CH–1211 Geneva
    Switzerland

European Computer Manufacturers' Association (ECMA)
    114 rue de Rhone
    CH–1204 Geneva
    Switzerland

For International Standard Book Numbers (ISBN):

International ISBN Agency
    c/o Staatsbibliothek Preussischer Kulturbesitz

Postfach 1047
D-1000 Berlin 30
Federal Republic of Germany

Standard Book Numbering Agency
12 Dyott Street
London WC1A 1DE
United Kingdom

Standard Book Number Agency
245 West 17th Street
New York NY 10011
United States of America

For International Standard Serials Numbers (ISSN):

International Serials Data System (ISDS)
International Centre
20 rue de Bachaumont
75002 Paris
France

UK National Serials Data Centre
Bibliographic Services
The British Library
2 Sheraton Street
London W1V 4BH
United Kingdom

National Serials Data Program
The Library of Congress
Washington DC 20540
United States of America

For Cataloguing-in-Publication (CIP):

CIP Development Officer
Cataloguing-in-Publication Programme

Useful Addresses

    Bibliographic Services
    The British Library
    2 Sheraton Street
    London W1V 4BH
    United Kingdom

Cataloguing-in-Publication Division
    Processing Services
    The Library of Congress
    Washington DC 20540
    United States of America

For legal deposit and copyright problems:

Copyright Receipt Office
    The British Library
    2 Sheraton Street
    London W1V 4BH
    United Kingdom

The Agent for the Copyright Libraries
(Mr A. T. Smail)
    100 Euston Street
    London NW1 2HQ
    United Kingdom

The British Copyright Council
    Copyright House
    29–33 Berners Street
    London W1P 4AA
    United Kingdom

Deposits and Acquisitions Division (LM 438E)
Copyright Office
    The Library of Congress
    Washington DC 20540
    United States of America

Author's choice

Not necessarily in the editions listed in the Guide:

The new Collins concise dictionary		26
The Oxford reference dictionary		28
Roget's Thesaurus		29
The Penguin modern guide to synonyms and related words		30
Partridge	Usage and abusage	33
Gowers	The complete plain words	34
Leech	A communicative grammar of English	41
The Economist pocket style book		124
O'Connor	Editing scientific books and journals	129
Martinsson	Guide for the preparation of scientific papers for publication	140
Unesco	The ABC of copyright	167
Dear	Oxford English	229

The specialist publications:

The ALA glossary of library and information science	65
ISO Standards Handbook 1: Information transfer	23
ISO Standards Handbook 10: Data processing – Vocabulary	18

Some general reference books including varying editions of:

> Brewer's dictionary of phrase and fable. Revised edition by Ivor H. Evans
> The Oxford dictionary of quotations
> Pears Cyclopaedia
> The Times concise atlas of the world

Some reflections on the English language:

> Howard, Philip The state of the language: English observed (Penguin Books, 1984)

And a wide variety of other personal favourites...

Index of topics and organizations

Abbreviations, in text 19, 21, 56
Abstracting and indexing services 21, 56, 57, 96
Abstracts, in publications 56, 57
Accompanying materials 99, 100
Acronyms, in text 19, 20, 56
American National Standards Institute (ANSI) 131
Analytic, defined 45
Appendices, in publications 57
Articles, in serials 25, 45, 58
Audio-visual aids 33, 34, 100, 101

Bibliographic references, in text 21, 58
Bibliographies, in publications 58
Binding operations 94, 95
Book trade 34, 61, 63, 68, 71, 72
British Copyright Council 135
British Library (CIP, Copyright, Serials) 134, 135
British Standards Institution xii, 131

Camera-ready copy 35, 73, 89
Cataloguing-in-publication (CIP) 55, 61, 63, 64, 134, 135
Committee on Data for Science and Technology (CODATA) 36, 37, 38
Component part, defined 45, 46
Computer output microfilm (COM) 98
Computers and computer applications 5, 7, 10, 70, 71, 73, 76, 80–5, 88, 89, 91, 93
Conferences 31, 32, 33
Consultative Committee of the International Telecommunications Union (CCITT) 84, 133
Copy editing 41, 46
Copyright requirements 55, 65, 66, 135
Corporate bodies as authors 54
Covers of publications 52, 59, 60
Creative editing 46, 47

Desk top publishing (DTP) 77, 92, 93, 94

139

Index

Dictionaries
  general 14, 15, 16
  multilingual 9, 10, 11, 33, 67, 79, 82
  specialist 27, 67, 80

Editing and editors
  changing role of editor 69–72
  and DTP 93
  editor as publisher 66, 67
  functions 41, 42, 46, 47
  in specific subject fields 47
European Computers' Manufacturers' Association (ECMA) 84, 133

Flow charts, in text 31
Forewords, in publications 55

Grammar textbooks 17

Illustrations, in text 29–31, 66
Indexes, in publications 58
Information technology 70–2, 85, 86
In-house printing 91, 92, 94
International Council of Scientific Unions (ICSU) 5, 36
International Electrotechnical Commission (IEC) 5, 24, 30, 83, 84, 133
International Information Centre for Terminology (Infoterm) 2, 6, 7, 133
International Organization for Standardization (ISO) x, xii, 2, 5, 8, 10, 36, 83, 84, 131
ISO Technical Committees
  ISO/TC6, Paper, board and pulps 87

ISO/TC10, Technical drawings 30
ISO/TC37, Terminology 5–10, 133
ISO/TC46, Documentation 6, 9, 10, 12, 69, 132
ISO/TC82, Mining 31
ISO/TC130, Graphic technology 67, 69, 87
ISO/TC145, Graphic symbols 30
ISO/TC171, Micrographics 97
International Serials Data System (ISDS) 22, 53, 61, 62, 134
International Standard Book Numbers (ISBN) 45, 46, 55, 60, 61, 62, 64, 65, 133, 134
International Standard Serial Numbers (ISSN) 22, 45, 46, 53, 55, 61, 62, 64, 134
International Union of Pure and Applied Chemistry (IUPAC) 5, 24, 30, 36

Key titles of serials 22, 45, 53, 62

Legal deposit requirements 60, 64, 65, 135
Library of Congress (US) (CIP, Copyright, Serials) 134, 135

Maps, in text 31
Microfiche 98, 99
Microfilming 97, 98
Microforms 71, 95, 96, 98, 99
Monograph defined 43–4
Monographic series defined 44

Index

Multilingual dictionaries 9, 10, 11, 33, 67, 79, 82
Multimedia publications 99, 100

Names of authors 53, 54
National Bureau of Standards (US) 38, 39, 132
National Information Standards Organization (US) 132
Notes, in text 58
Numbers, in text 22, 23, 24
Numeric data 35–9

Optical character recognition (OCR) 90

Paper 85, 87, 88
Photocomposition 89, 91
Prefaces in publications 55
Print specifications 86, 87
Printers for in-house operations 91, 92, 94
Printing design and technology 67, 68, 70, 71, 86–91, 94
Proofs and proof corrections 69, 70, 71
Publications
  bibliographic categories 42–6
  designing 86, 87
  elements making up 50–60
  multimedia 99, 100
Publishing and publishers
  author as publisher 34, 35, 69
  defined 74
  desk top publishing 77, 92, 93, 94
  editor as publisher 66, 67
  electronic publishing 80, 82
  general guides 34

legal requirements 55, 59, 60, 64, 65, 66
marketing 61, 63, 68, 71
new products 70, 71
specialized texts 47, 68
Punctuation 17, 18

Quotations, in text 18, 19, 65, 66

References, in publications 58
Report writng 25, 26

Serials
  choice of titles 53
  defined 44, 45
  identification, in references 58
  key titles 22, 45, 53, 62
  title abbreviations 21, 22
SI units 23
Spine titles 52
Spoken text 31–3
Statistical methods 24, 38
Style manuals
  editorial 47–9
  general 16, 17
  prepared by professional bodies 28, 29, 48, 49
  for special types of publications 25, 26, 49, 50
  in specific subject fields 27–9
Symbols in text 22–4, 30, 31

Tables, in text 30
Tables of contents, in publications 55, 56
Technical drawings, in text 30, 31
Terminology 3–11
Theses 25
Title pages, in publications 52–5

141

Index

Title pages verso, in publications 54, 55
Titles of publications 54
Translations identified, in publications 60
Transliteration 11, 12
Typewriters 73, 75, 76, 77
Typographic design 60, 67, 68, 86, 87

Unesco
  address 131, 132
  General Information Programme x, 132
  support for standards development x, 6, 8, 49, 50
  UNISIST Programme x, 6

UNISIST guide to standards for information handling x
United Nations 5
Units of measurement in text 22, 23

Word processors
  author as publisher 34, 35, 69
  development 73, 74
  use and advantages 76–81
World Health Organization 5
Written text
  illustrations in text 29–31
  preparation 13, 14
  for special types of publications 24, 25, 26
  in specific subject fields 26–9, 47